ANCIENT POEMS,

BALLADS, AND SONGS

OF THE

PEASANTRY OF ENGLAND

ANCIENT POEMS,

BALLADS, AND SONGS

OF THE

PEASANTRY OF ENGLAND,

TAKEN DOWN FROM ORAL RECITATION, AND TRANSCRIBED

FROM PRIVATE MANUSCRIPTS, RARE BROADSIDES,

AND SCARCE PUBLICATIONS.

———

COLLECTED, AND EDITED BY

JAMES HENRY DIXON.

———

"Our *English* lays! 'Tis even such a wreath
As may be gathered from the hedge-row banks,
When linnets sing, and all is glad in June.
'Tis even such! perchance of worthless weeds
'Twill seem, nor win one little day of smiles.
Yet frown not thou;—who mocks the legends hoar
Of olden time, or deems the minstrel song
An empty strain, or jingle of vain sounds,
Were better shunned than cherished!"
                                    KENNEDY.

———

EP PUBLISHING LIMITED
1973

Copyright © 1973 EP Publishing Limited
East Ardsley, Wakefield
Yorkshire, England.

First published by The Percy Society
(in Volume XVII of its publications),
London, 1846.

Reproduced from a copy of the first edition
kindly loaned by the University of
Bristol Library.

ISBN 0 85409 871 2

Please address all enquiries to EP Publishing Ltd.
(address as above)

Printed in Great Britain by
The Scolar Press Limited, Menston, Yorkshire.

PREFACE.

———

THE present work is a selection from the poetry of our peasantry, and the Editor trusts that the publication, albeit an humble one, may not be deemed an unacceptable New-Year's offering to the PERCY SOCIETY.

He who, in travelling through the rural districts of England, has made the road-side inn his resting place,—who has visited the lowly dwellings of the villagers and yeomanry, and been present at their feasts and festivals, must have observed that there are certain old poems, ballads and songs which are favourites with the masses, and have been said and sung from generation to generation. Though, for a time, popular modern compositions may obscure their lustre, the new publications have only an ephemeral existence, and the peasantry go back to their antiquated favourites, remarking, that " the old rhymes are the best, after all !" This veneration for antiquity was, at one time, in imminent danger of being destroyed by the prevalence of that Utilitarian spirit which, seeking to turn every thing it touches into gold, would invade the realms of Fancy and Romance, banish the bright day-dreams of our youth, and leave us nothing but a cold Saducean philosophy in its stead. The anti-quarian world, however, at the present period, witnesses the dawning of a brighter day, and in several of the recent serial publications, popular treatises on subjects connected with religion and science are found in close companionship with heart-stirring descriptions of rural games and pas-times, with nursery rhymes, with fairy legends, and romantic ballads. But amid all this growing fondness for the relics of a by-gone age, there is one description of literature which does not seem to us to have received that attention which its merits warrant,—and that is the poetry of our pea-santry ; the literature which, however despised by some, is, nevertheless, the source from whence was derived the first inspired breathings of a Burns, a Bloomfield, and a Clare ; the only profane literature, indeed, with which, until a very recent period, the cottager was acquainted, and which shared his humble book-shelf, with his *Pilgrim's Progress*, and other so-called " godly books."

Our publication, although far exceeding the limits we originally intended, only exhibits a *few* specimens of peasant-rhymes collected by us; for, during the progress of the work, the *matériel* has so increased under our own hands, and been so swelled by contributions from every part of the country, that we have been necessitated to omit much that is curious and interesting. In what we have retained, however, will be found every variety,

" From gay to grave, from lively to severe,"

from the moral poem and the religious dialogue,—

" The scrolls that teach us to live and to die,"

to the legendary, the historical, or the domestic ballad; from the strains that enliven the harvest-home and festival, to the love-ditties which the country-lass warbles, or the comic song with which the rustic sets the village hostel in a roar.

In our Collection are several pieces exceedingly scarce, and hitherto only to be met with in broadsides and chap-books of the utmost rarity; in

addition to which we have given several others
never before in print, and obtained by the Editor
and his friends, either from the oral recitation of
the peasantry, or from manuscripts in the possession of private individuals.

Nor will there be discovered in our pages a
solitary "modern antique," or literary forgery;
and, with the exception of two provincial-songs,
being those respectively numbered xxvi. and
xxvii., and the sea-song numbered xxxix. — and
even these are strains of a by-passed time,—there
is not a single insertion which is not justly entitled to the epithet *old*, if not to that of *ancient*.

Amongst the friends who have assisted us by
their contributions and remarks, we must not
forget to name W. H. Ainsworth, Esq., Wm.
Chappell, Esq., F.S.A., T. Crofton Croker, Esq.,
F. W. Fairholt, Esq., F.S.A., J. S. Moore, Esq.,
Dr. Rimbault, F.S.A., Wm. Sandys, Esq., F.S.A.,
and Thomas Wright, Esq., M.A., the Secretary to
the Percy Society.   To the above gentlemen our
thanks are especially due, as well as to several
correspondents moving in a humbler sphere.

As a parting word, we would express a hope
that if our work should fall into the hands of any

who may hitherto have regarded the literary *parterre* of the English peasant as a rank and unweeded garden, a kind glance may be bestowed on the flowers we have culled while hastily passing through it. If they be not so stately in appearance, and so brilliant in tint, as those growing in more favoured situations, and cultivated under happier auspices, they may, perchance, be found to form a not unlovely "garland," although, to use the language of Shelley, it be composed only of the—

> ———" flowers
> That bloom in mossy banks and darksome glens,
> Lighting the green-wood with their sunny smiles."

J. H. D.

Tollington Villa,
   Hornsey.

CONTENTS.

POEMS.

BALLADS.

SONGS.

SONGS IN THE NOTES.

ANCIENT POEMS, BALLADS, &c.

POEMS.

I.

The Vanities of Life.

THE following verses were copied by John Clare, the Northamptonshire peasant, from a M.S. on the fly-leaves of an old book in the possession of a poor man, and entitled " *The World's best Wealth; a Collection of choice Councils in Verse and Prose. Printed for A. Bettesworth, at the Red Lion in Paternoster-row*, 1720." They were in a "crabbed, quaint hand, and difficult to decypher." Clare remitted the poem to Montgomery, the author of " *The World before the Flood*," &c. &c., by whom it was published in the *Sheffield Iris*. Montgomery's criticism is as follows:—" long as the poem appears to the eye, it will abundantly repay the pleasure of perusal, being full of condensed and admirable thought, as well as diversified with exuberant imagery, and embellished with peculiar felicity of language: the moral points in the closing couplets of the stanzas are often powerfully enforced." The editor thinks that most readers will agree in the justice of Montgomery's remarks. He has not been able to discover any old printed copy of the poem, which, as Clare supposes, was probably written about the commencement of the 18th century; the unknown author appears to have been a person deeply imbued with the spirit and train of thought of the popular devotional writers of the preceding century, as Herbert, Quarles, &c., but

B

who had modelled his smoother and more elegant versification after that of the poetic school of his own times.

———

Vanity of vanities, all is vanity."—SOLOMON.

WHAT are life's joys and gains?
    What pleasures crowd its ways,
That man should take such pains
    To seek them all his days?
Sift this untoward strife
    On which thy mind is bent,
See if this chaff of life
    Is worth the trouble spent.

Is pride thy heart's desire?
    Is power thy climbing aim?
Is love thy folly's fire?
    Is wealth thy restless game?
Pride, power, love, wealth and all,
    Time's touchstone shall destroy,
And, like base coin, prove all
    Vain substitutes for joy.

Dost think that pride exalts
    Thyself in others eyes,
And hides thy folly's faults,
    Which reason will despise?
Dost strut, and turn, and stride,
    Like walking weather-cocks?
The shadow by thy side
    Becomes thy ape, and mocks.

Dost think that power's disguise
   Can make thee mighty seem?
It may in folly's eyes,
   But not in worth's esteem:
When all that thou canst ask,
   And all that she can give,
Is but a paltry mask
   Which tyrants wear and live.

Go, let thy fancies range
   And ramble where they may;
View power in every change,
   And what is the display?
—The country magistrate,
   The lowest shade in power,
To rulers of the state,
   The meteors of an hour:—

View all, and mark the end
   Of every proud extreme,
Where flattery turns a friend,
   And counterfeits esteem;
Where worth is aped in show,
   That doth her name purloin,
Like toys of golden glow
   That's sold for copper coin.

Ambition's haughty nod,
   With fancies may deceive,
Nay, tell thee thou'rt a god,—
   And wilt thou such believe?

Go, bid the seas be dry,
　Go, hold earth like a ball,
Or throw her fancies by,
　For God can do it all.

Dost thou possess the dower
　Of laws to spare or kill?
Call it not heav'nly power
　When but a tyrant's will;
Know what a God will do,
　And know thyself a fool,
Nor tyrant-like pursue
　Where He alone should rule.

Dost think, when wealth is won,
　Thy heart has its desire?
Hold ice up to the sun,
　And wax before the fire;
Nor triumph o'er the reign
　Which they so soon resign;
In this world weigh the gain,
　Insurance safe is thine.

Dost think life's peace secure
　In houses and in land?
Go, read the fairy lure
　To twist a cord of sand,
Lodge stones upon the sky,
　Hold water in a sieve,
Nor give such tales the lie,
　And still thine own believe.

Whoso with riches deals,
   And thinks peace bought and sold,
Will find them slippery eels,
   That slide the firmest hold :
Though sweet as sleep with health,
   Thy lulling luck may be,
Pride may o'erstride thy wealth,
   And check prosperity.

Dost think that beauty's power,
   Life's sweetest pleasure gives ?
Go, pluck the summer flower,
   And see how long it lives:
Behold, the rays glide on,
   Along the summer plain,
Ere thou canst say, " they're gone,"
   And measure beauty's reign.

Look on the brightest eye,
   Nor teach it to be proud,
But view the clearest sky
   And thou shalt find a cloud;
Nor call each face ye meet
   An angel's, 'cause it's fair,
But look beneath your feet,
   And think of what ye are.

Who thinks that love doth live
   In beauty's tempting show,
Shall find his hopes ungive,
   And melt in reason's thaw ;

Who thinks that pleasure lies
　In every fairy bower,
Shall oft, to his surprise,
　Find poison in the flower.

Dost lawless pleasures grasp ?
　Judge not thou deal'st in joy;
Its flowers but hide the asp,
　Thy revels to destroy:
Who trusts an harlot's smile,
　And by her wiles is led,
Plays with a sword the while,
　Hung dropping o'er his head.

Dost doubt my warning song?
　Then doubt the sun gives light,
Doubt truth to teach thee wrong,
　And wrong alone as right;
And live as lives the knave,
　Intrigue's deceiving guest,
Be tyrant, or be slave,
　As suits thy ends the best.

Or pause amid thy toils,
　For visions won and lost,
And count the fancied spoils,
　If e'er they quit the cost ;
And if they still possess
　Thy mind, as worthy things,
Pick straws with Bedlam Bess,
　And call them diamond rings.

Thy folly 's past advice,
   Thy heart 's already won,
Thy fall 's above all price,
   So go, and be undone;
For all who thus prefer
   The seeming great for small,
Shall make wine vinegar,
   And sweetest honey gall.

Wouldst heed the truths I sing,
   To profit wherewithall,
Clip folly's wanton wing,
   And keep her within call :
I've little else to give,
   What thou canst easy try,
The lesson how to live,
   Is but to learn to die.

———

II.

The Life and Age of Man.

FROM one of Thackeray's Catalogues, preserved in the British
Museum, it appears that "*The Life and Age of Man*" was one
of the productions printed by him at the " Angel in Duck Lane,
London." Thackeray's imprint is found attached to broadsides
published between 1672 and 1688. The present reprint, the
correctness of which is very questionable, is taken from a modern
broadside. The editor has to express his regret, that he has not
been able to meet with any older edition.

———

IN prime of years, when I was young.
I took delight in youthful ways,

Not knowing then what did belong
    Unto the pleasures of those days.
At seven years old I was a child,
And subject then to be beguil'd.

At two times seven I went to learn
    What discipline is taught at school:
When good from ill I could discern,
    I thought myself no more a fool:
My parents were contriving plan,
How I might live when I were man.

At three times seven I waxèd wild,
    When manhood led me to be bold;
I thought myself no more a child,
    My own conceit it so me told:
Then did I venture far and near,
To buy delight at price full dear.

At four times seven I take a wife,
    And leave off all my wanton ways,
Thinking thereby perhaps to thrive,
    And save myself from sad disgrace.
So farewell my companions all,
For other business doth me call.

At five times seven I must hard strive,
    What I could gain by mighty skill;
But still against the stream I drive,

And bowl up stones against the hill;
The more I labor'd might and main,
The more I strove against the stream.

At six times seven all covetise
   Began to harbour in my breast;
My mind still then contriving was
   How I might gain this worldly wealth;
To purchase lands and live on them,
So make my children mighty men.

At seven times seven all worldly thought
   Began to harbour in my brain;
Then did I drink a heavy draught
   Of water of experience plain;
There none so ready was as I,
To purchase bargains, sell, or buy.

At eight times seven I waxèd old,
   And took myself unto my rest,
Neighbours then sought my counsel bold,
   And I was held in great request;
But age did so abate my strength,
That I was forc'd to yield at length.

At nine times seven take my leave
   Of former vain delights must I;
It then full sorely did me grieve—
   I fetchèd many a heavy sigh;
To rise up early, and sit up late,
My former life, I loathe and hate.

At ten times seven my glass is run,
    And I poor silly man must die;
I lookèd up and saw the sun,
    Had overcome the crystal sky.
So now I must this world forsake,
Another man my place must take.

Now you may see, as in a glass,
    The whole estate of mortal men;
How they from seven to seven do pass,
    Untill they are threescore and ten;
And when their glass is fully run,
They must leave off as they begun.

III.

The Young Man's Wish.

FROM an old copy, without printer's name, in possession of the editor: probably one from the Aldermary Church-yard press. Poems in triplets were very popular during the reign of Charles I, as also during the Interregnum, and the reign of Charles II.

IF I could but attain my wish,
I'd have each day one wholesome dish,
Of plain meat, or fowl, or fish.

A glass of port, with good old beer,
In winter time a fire burnt clear,
Tobacco, pipes, an easy chair.

In some clean town a snug retreat,
A little garden 'fore my gate,
With thousand pounds a year estate.

After my house expense was clear,
Whatever I could have to spare,
The neighb'ring poor should freely share.

To keep content and peace through life,
I'd have a prudent cleanly wife,
Stranger to noise, and eke to strife.

Then I, when blest with such estate,
With such an house, and such a mate,
Would envy not the worldly great.

Let them for noisy honours try,
Let them seek worldly praise, while I
Unnoticèd would live and die.

But since dame Fortune 's not thought fit
To place me in affluence, yet,
I'll be content with what I get.

He 's happiest far whose humble mind,
Is unto Providence resign'd,
And thinketh fortune always kind.

Then I will strive to bound my wish,
And take, instead of fowl and fish,
Whate'er is thrown into my dish.

Instead of wealth and fortune great,
Garden and house and loving mate,
I'll rest content in servile state.

I'll from each folly strive to fly,
Each virtue to attain I'll try,
And live as I would wish to die.

————

IV.

𝕿𝖍𝖊 𝕸𝖎𝖉𝖓𝖎𝖌𝖍𝖙 𝕸𝖊𝖘𝖘𝖊𝖓𝖌𝖊𝖗:

OR A SUDDEN CALL FROM AN EARTHLY GLORY TO THE
COLD GRAVE.

In a Dialogue between Death, and a Rich Man; who, in the midst
of all his Wealth, received the tidings of his Last Day, to
his unspeakable and sorrowful Lamentation.

To the tune of "*Aim not too high,*" &c.

————

THE following poem, as also those numbered V and VI, belongs
to a class of publications which have ever been peculiar favourites
with the poor, in whose cottages they may be frequently seen,
neatly framed and glazed, and suspended from the white-washed
wall. They belong to the school of Quarles, and can be traced
to the time when that writer was in the height of his popularity.
These religious dialogues are numerous, but the majority of them

are very namby-pamby productions, and unworthy of a reprint.
The modern editions preserve the old form of the broadside of
the seventeenth century, and are *adorned* with rude woodcuts,
probably copies of the original ones—

> ———— " wooden cuts
> Strange, and uncouth ; dire faces, figures dire,
> Sharp-knee'd, sharp-elbowed, and lean ancled too,
> With long and ghostly shanks, forms which once seen,
> Can never be forgotten !"—*Wordsworth's Excursion.*

DEATH.

THOU wealthy man of large possessions here,
Amounting to some thousand pounds a year,
Extorted by oppression from the poor,
The time is come that thou shalt be no more;
Thy house therefore in order set with speed,
And call to mind how you your life do lead,
Let true repentance be thy chiefest care,
And for another world now, *now* prepare;
For notwithstanding all your heaps of gold,
Your lands and lofty buildings manifold,
Take notice you must die this very day,
And therefore kiss your bags and come away.

RICH MAN.

(He started straight and turn'd his head aside,
Where seeing pale fac'd Death, aloud he cried),
Lean famish'd slave! why do you threaten so,
Whence come you, pray, and whither must I go?

DEATH.

I come from ranging round the universe,
Thro' courts and kingdoms far and near I pass,

Where rich and poor, distressèd, bond and free,
Fall soon or late a sacrifice to me.
From crownèd Kings to captives bound in chains
My power reaches, sir; the longest reigns
That ever were, I put a period to;
And now I'm come in fine to conquer you.

RICH MAN.

I can't nor won't believe that you, pale Death,
Were sent this day to stop my vital breath,
By reason I in perfect health remain,
Free from diseases, sorrow, grief, and pain;
No heavy heart, nor fainting fits have I,
And do you say that I am drawing nigh
The latter minute? sure it cannot be;
Depart therefore, you are not sent for me.

DEATH.

Yes, yes, I am, for did you never know,
The tender grass and pleasant flowers that grow
Perhaps one minute, are the next cut down,
And so is man, tho' fam'd with high renown?
Have you not heard the doleful passing bell
Ring out for those that were alive and well
The other day, in health and pleasure too,
And had as little thoughts of death as you?
For let me tell you, when my warrant's seal'd,
The sweetest beauty that the earth doth yield
At my approach shall turn as pale as lead;
'Tis I that lay them on their dying bed.

I kill with dropsy, phthisick, stone, and gout;
But when my raging fevers fly about,
I strike the man, perhaps, but over-night,
Who hardly lives to see the morning light;
I'm sent each hour, like to a nimble page,
To infant, hoary heads, and middle age;
Time after time I sweep the world quite thro';
Then it's in vain to think I'll favour you.

RICH MAN.

Proud Death, you see what awful sway I bear,
For when I frown none of my servants dare
Approach my presence, but in corners hide
Until I am appeas'd and pacified.
Nay, men of greater rank I keep in awe
Nor did I ever fear the force of law,
But ever did my enemies subdue,
And must I after all submit to you?

DEATH.

'Tis very true, for why thy daring soul,
Which never could endure the least controul,
I'll thrust thee from this earthly tenement,
And thou shalt to another world be sent.

RICH MAN.

What! must I die and leave a vast estate,
Which, with my gold, I purchas'd but of late?
Besides what I had many years ago?—
What! must my wealth and I be parted so?

If you your darts and arrows must let fly,
Go search the jails, where mourning debtors lie;
Release them from their sorrow, grief, and woe,
For I am rich and therefore loath to go.

DEATH

I'll search no jails, but the right mark I'll hit;
And though you are unwilling to submit,
Yet die you must, no other friend can do,—
Prepare yourself to go, I'm come for you.
If you had all the world and ten times more,
Yet die you must,—there's millions gone before;
The greatest kings on earth yield and obey,
And at my feet their crowns and sceptres lay:
If crownèd heads and right renownèd peers
Die in the prime and blossoms of their years,
Can you suppose to gain a longer space?
No! I will send you to another place.

RICH MAN.

Oh! stay thy hand and be not so severe,
I have a hopeful son and daughter dear,
All that I beg is but to let me live
That I may them in lawful marriage give:
They being young when I am laid in the grave,
I fear they will be wrong'd of what they have:
Altho' of me you will no pity take,
Yet spare me for my little infants' sake.

DEATH.

If such a vain excuse as this might do,
It would be long e'er mortals would go thro

The shades of death; for every man would find
Something to say that he might stay behind.
Yet, if ten thousand arguments they'd use,
The destiny of dying to excuse,
They'll find it is in vain with me to strive,
For why, I part the dearest friends alive;
Poor parents die, and leave their children small
With nothing to support them here withall,
But the kind hand of gracious Providence,
Who is their father, friend, and sole defence.
Tho' I have held you long in disrepute,
Yet after all here with a sharp salute
I'll put a period to your days and years,
Causing your eyes to flow with dying tears.

RICH MAN.

(Then with a groan he made this sad complaint):
My heart is dying, and my spirits faint;
To my close chamber let me be convey'd;
Farewell, false world, for thou hast me betray'd.
Would I had never wrong'd the fatherless,
Nor mourning widows when in sad distress;
Would I had ne'er been guilty of that sin,
Would I had never known what gold had been;
For by the same my heart was drawn away
To search for gold: but now this very day,
I find it is but like a slender reed,
Which fails me most when most I stand in need;
For, woe is me! the time is come at last,
Now I am on a bed of sorrow cast,

C

Where in lamenting tears I weeping lie,
Because my sins make me afraid to die:
Oh! Death, be pleas'd to spare me yet awhile,
That I to God myself may reconcile,
For true repentance some small time allow,
I never fear'd a future state till now,
My bags of gold and land I'd freely give,
For to obtain the favour here to live,
Until I have a sure foundation laid.
Let me not die before my peace be made!

DEATH.

Thou hast not many minutes here to stay,
Lift up your heart to God without delay,
Implore his pardon now for what is past,
Who knows but he may save your soul at last?

RICH MAN.

I'll water now with tears my dying bed,
Before the Lord my sad complaint I'll spread,
And if he will vouchsafe to pardon me,
To die and leave this world I could be free.
False world! false world, farewell! farewell! adieu!
I find, I find, there is no trust in you!
For when upon a dying bed we lie,
Your gilded baits are nought but misery.
My youthful son and loving daughter dear,
Take warning by your dying father here;
Let not the world deceive you at this rate,
For fear a sad repentance comes too late.

Sweet babes, I little thought the other day,
I should so suddenly be snatch'd away
By Death, and leave you weeping here behind;
But life's a most uncertain thing, I find.
When in the grave my head is lain full low,
Pray let not folly prove your overthrow;
Serve ye the Lord, obey his holy will,
That he may have a blessing for you still.
(Having saluted them, he turned aside,
These were the very words before he died):

> A painful life I ready am to leave,
> Wherefore, in mercy, Lord, my soul receive.

V.

A Dialogue betwixt an Exciseman and Death.

TRANSCRIBED from a printed copy in the British Museum. The
idea of Death being employed to execute a writ, reminds the
editor of an epitaph which he met with in a village church-yard
at the foot of the Wrekin, in Shropshire, and which commenced
thus:—

> " The King of Heaven a warrant got,
>   And seal'd it without delay,
>   And he did give the same to Death,
>   For him to serve straightway." &c. &c.

UPON a time when Titan's steeds were driven
To drench themselves beneath the western heaven;

c 2

And sable Morpheus had his curtains spread,
And silent night had laid the world to bed,
'Mongst other night-birds which did seek for prey,
A blunt exciseman, which abhorr'd the day,
Was rambling forth to seeke himself a booty
'Mongst merchant's goods which had not paid the duty:
But walking all alone, Death chanc'd to meet him,
And in this manner did begin to greet him.

DEATH.

Stand, who comes here? what means this knave to
      peepe
And sculke abroad, when honest men should sleepe?
Speake, what's thy name? and quickly tell me this,
Whither thou goest, and what thy bus'ness is?

EXCISEMAN.

Whate'er my bus'ness is, thou foule-mouth'd scould,
I'de have you know I scorn to be controul'd
By any man that lives; much less by thou,
Who blurtest out thou knowst not what, nor how;
I goe about my lawful bus'ness; and
I'le make you smarte for bidding of mee stand.

DEATH.

Imperious cox-combe! is your stomach vext?
Pray slack your rage, and harken what comes next:
I have a writt to take you up; therefore,
To chafe your blood, I bid you stand, once more.

EXCISEMAN.

A writt to take *mee* up! excuse mee, sir,
You doe mistake, I am an officer
In publick service, for my private wealth;
My bus'ness is, if any seeke by stealth
To undermine the states, I doe discover
Their falsehood; therefore hold your hand,—give over.

DEATH.

Nay, fair and soft! 'tis not so quickly done
As you conceive it is: I am not gone
A jott the sooner, for your hastie chat
Nor bragging language; for I tell you flat
'Tis more then so, though fortune seeme to thwart us,
Such easie terms I don't intend shall part us.
With this impartial arme I'll make you feele
My fingers first, and with this shaft of steele
I'le peck thy bones ! *as thou alive wert hated,*
So dead, to doggs thou shalt be segregated.

EXCISEMAN.

I'de laugh at that; I would thou didst but dare
To lay thy fingers on me ; I'de not spare
To hack thy carkass till my sword was broken,
I'de make thee eat the wordes which thou hast spoken;
All men should warning take by thy transgression,
How they molested men of my profession.
My service to the states is so welle known,
That should I but complaine, they'd quickly owne

My publicke grievances; and give mee right
To cut your eares, before to-morrow night.

DEATH.

Well said indeed! but bootless all, for I
Am well acquainted with thy villanie;
I know thy office, and thy trade is such,
Thy service little, and thy gaines are much:
Thy braggs are many; but 'tis vaine to swagger,
And thinke to fighte mee with thy guilded dagger:
As I abhor thy person, place, and threate,
So now I'le bring thee to the judgement seate.

EXCISEMAN.

The judgement seate! I must confess that word
Doth cut my heart, like any sharpnèd sword:
What! come t' account! methinks the dreadful sound
Of every word doth make a mortal wound,
Which sticks not only in my outward skin,
But penetrates my very soule within.
'Twas least of all my thoughts that ever Death
Would once attempt to stop excisemen's breath.
But since 'tis so, that now I doe perceive
You are in earnest, then I must relieve
Myself another way: come, wee'l be friends,
If I have wrongèd thee, I'le make th' amendes.
Let's joyne together; I'le pass my word this night
Shall yield us grub, before the morning light.
Or otherwise, (to mitigate my sorrow),
Stay here, I'le bring you gold enough to-morrow.

DEATH.

To-morrow's gold I will not have; and thou
Shalt have no gold upon to-morrow: now
My final writt shall to th' execution have thee,
All earthly treasure cannot help or save thee.

EXCISEMAN.

Then woe is mee! ah! how was I befool'd!
I thought that gold, (which answereth all things) could
Have stood my friend at any time to baile mee!
But griefe growes great, and now my trust doth faile
     me.
Oh! that my conscience were but clear within,
Which now is rackèd with my former sin;
With horror I behold my secret stealing,
My bribes, oppression, and my graceless dealing;
My office-sins, which I had clean forgotten,
Will gnaw my soul when all my bones are rotten:
I must confess it, very griefe doth force mee,
Dead or alive, both God and man doth curse mee.
Let all Excisemen hereby warning take,
To shun their practice for their conscience sake.

FINIS.

London: printed by I. C[larke], 1659.

VI.

The Messenger of Mortality:

Or Life and Death contrasted in a Dialogue betwixt Death and a Lady.

ONE of the most beautiful and plaintive poems of "Elia," (Charles Lamb), was suggested by this old dialogue. The tune is given in Chappell's "*National English Airs.*" In Carey's "*Musical Century,*" 1738, it is called the "Old tune of *Death and the Lady.*" The four concluding lines of the present copy of "*Death and the Lady*" are found inscribed on tomb-stones in village church-yards in every part of England. They are not, however, contained in an old broadside edition now in the possession of Dr. Rimbault, and with which our reprint has been carefully collated.

———

DEATH.

FAIR lady, lay your costly robes aside,
No longer may you glory in your pride;
Take leave of all your carnal vain delight,
I'm come to summon you away this night!

LADY.

What bold attempt is this? pray let me know
From whence you come, and whither I must go?
Must I, who am a lady, stoop or bow
To such a pale-fac'd visage? Who art thou?

DEATH.

Do you not know me? well! I tell thee, then,
It's I that conquer all the sons of men!
No pitch of honour from my dart is free;
My name is Death! have you not heard of me?

LADY.

Yes! I have heard of thee time after time,
But being in the glory of my prime,

I did not think you would have call'd so soon.
Why must my morning sun go down at noon?

DEATH.

Talk not of noon! you may as well be mute;
This is no time at all for to dispute:
Your riches, garments, gold, and jewels brave,
Houses and lands must all new owners have;
Tho' thy vain heart to riches was inclin'd,
Yet thou must die and leave them all behind.

LADY.

My heart is cold; I tremble at the news;
There's bags of gold, if thou wilt me excuse,
And seize on them, and finish thou the strife
Of those that are aweary of their life.
Are there not many bound in prison strong,
In bitter grief of soul have languish'd long,
Who could but find a grave a place of rest,
From all the grief in which they are opprest?
Besides, there's many with a hoary head,
And palsy joints, by which their joys are fled;
Release thou them whose sorrows are so great,
But spare my life to have a longer date?

DEATH.

Tho' some by age be full of grief and pain,
Yet their appointed time they must remain:
I come to none before their warrant's seal'd,
And when it is, they must submit and yield.
I take no bribe, believe me, this is true;
Prepare yourself to go; I'm come for you.

LADY.

Death, be not so severe, let me obtain
A little longer time to live and reign !
Fain would I stay if thou my life will spare;
I have a daughter beautiful and fair,
I'd live to see her wed whom I adore:
Grant me but this and I will ask no more.

DEATH.

This is a slender frivolous excuse;
I have you fast, and will not let you loose;
Leave her to Providence, for you must go
Along with me, whether you will or no;
I, Death, command the King to leave his crown,
And at my feet he lays his sceptre down!
Then if to kings I don't this favor give,
But cut them off, can you expect to live
Beyond the limits of your time and space?
No! I must send you to another place.

LADY.

You learned doctors, now express your skill,
And let not Death of me obtain his will ;
Prepare your cordials, let me comfort find,
My gold shall fly like chaff before the wind.

DEATH.

Forbear to call, their skill will never do,
They are but mortals here as well as you:
I give the fatal wound, my dart is sure,

And far beyond the doctor's skill to cure.
How freely can you let your riches fly
To purchase life, rather than yield to die!
But while you flourish here with all your store,
You will not give one penny to the poor;
Tho' in God's name their suit to you they make,
You would not spare one penny for his sake!
The Lord beheld wherein you did amiss,
And calls you hence to give account for this!

LADY.

Oh! heavy news! must I no longer stay?
How shall I stand in the great judgment day?
(Down from her eyes the chrystal tears did flow:
She said), none knows what I do undergo:
Upon my bed of sorrow here I lie;
My carnal life makes me afraid to die.
My sins alas! are many, gross, and foul,
Oh righteous Lord! have mercy on my soul!
And tho' I do deserve thy righteous frown,
Yet pardon, Lord, and pour a blessing down.
(Then with a dying sigh her heart did break,
And did the pleasures of this world forsake).

———

Thus may we see the high and mighty fall,
For cruel Death shews no respect at all
To any one of high or low degree,
Great men submit to Death as well as we.
Tho' they are gay, their life is but a span—
A lump of clay—so vile a creature's man.

Then happy those whom Christ has made his care,
Who die in the Lord, and ever blessed are.
The grave's the market place where all men meet,
Both rich and poor, as well as small and great.
If life were merchandize that gold could buy,
The rich would live, the poor alone would die.

VII.

The Weaver's Garland.

Or a New School for Christian Patience.

FROM an inquiry into the origin of these verses, the editor is in-clined to fix the date about the year 1700-1, a few years after the passing of the " Lustring act," when, in consequence of a change of fashion, there was a panic in the silk trade, and the weavers of Spitalfields were reduced to a state of the greatest distress. During other panics in the same trade, it has been customary with the London ballad-printers to reprint the Garland, and for the weavers, accompanied by their wives and families to recite it in the streets. It was originally printed at the Aldermary Church-yard press. The last edition was issued a few years ago in the old broadside form, by the late Mr. Pitts, of Great St. Andrew's Street, London, whose copy was an exact transcript from one printed by Marshall, his predecessor.

SWEET, dear, and loving wife!
My senses are at strife,
About this careful life,
   For we decline:

Times being grievous hard,
All trading spoil'd and marr'd,
I have a sweet regard
   For thee and thine.

I thank you for your care,
Yet, husband! don't despair,
Let us with patience bear,
   These troubles here:
Dear love! 'tis all in vain
To weep, sigh, and complain,
Love, we may thrive again,
   Be of good cheer.

My dearest love! said he,
How can I cheerful be,
While pinching poverty
   Knocks at the door?
And will not hence depart,
But wounds me to the heart;
I never felt such smart,
   Sweet wife, before.

Dear husband, do not make
Such moan, for heaven's sake!
Of me this council take,
   Your bosom friend:
By patience put your trust
In Him that made you first,
When times are at the worst
   Sure they will mend.

Dear love! it may be so,
But while the grass doth grow
The steed may starve, you know,
    Then 'tis too late;
So my dear family,
Which wants a quick supply,
By long delays may die,
    O cruel fate!

Sweet husband! don't despair,
Avoid distracting care,
I will the burden bear
    Along with you:
Our sons and daughters they
Shall work, and if we may
Get bread from day to day,
    Love! that will do.

At a sad dismal rate,
Sweet wife, thou know'st of late
My losses have been great,
    By wicked men.
Pine not for worldly pelf,
Bless God we have our health,
And that is more than wealth,
    Be thankful, then.

Job lost abundance more,
Besides his body sore,
Yet he with patience bore,
    While tidings came,

How all in ruins lay:
He patiently did say,
God gives and takes away,
   Blest be his name.

Job did not fume and fret,
When with these things he met,
Dear loving husband! let
   Us imitate
His patience, while in pain;
Job found it not in vain,
God rais'd him up again,
   And made him great.

Love! I have often read
How Job was comforted,
Yet I am full of dread,
   And fear, for why?
Our family is large,
Six children are some charge,
We fall within the verge
   Of poverty.

Dear husband! don't repine,
Nor grudge this charge of mine;
Blest be the powers divine,
   Sweet babes they are.
When we shall aged grow,
With locks like winter snow,
They may, for ought I know,
   Lessen our care.

It is a great offence,
To distrust Providence,
Whose blessed influence,
    Takes special care
Of all the sons of men.
Husband! be cheerful then,
God will be gracious when
    Thankful we are.

My fingers do not itch
To be exceeding rich,
May we but get thro' stitch,
    Keep from the door
The greedy wolf of prey,
And all our dealers pay,
Believe me what I say,
    We need no more.

I and my children dear,
Will work then; never fear
But we shall something clear.
    Tommy shall weave,
The girls shall all begin,
Forthwith to card and spin,
Which will bring something in:
    Then never grieve.

Those hands that never wrought
Shall be to labour brought,
All which I never thought
    Would be, till now;

But in regard I see
It is my destiny,
I'll draw along with thee,
   God speed the PLOUGH.

I value not to dine
On sumptuous dishes fine,
With rich and racy wine
   From foreign parts:
Good wholesome bread and beer
Instead of better cheer,
Let us receive, my dear,
   With thankful hearts.

In all conditions still,
Let us not take it ill,
Since 'tis his blessed will,
   It should be so;
Whether we rise or fall,
Our substance great or small,
Content is all in all,
   My dear! you know.

O most indulgent mate!
After this long debate,
My comforts they are great,
   In a kind wife.
Tho' some may think it strange,
My fancy seem'd to range,
But now a happy change,
   Doth bless my life.

D

For to my joy I find
A sweet composèd mind,
I wish that all mankind,
  Was full as well ;
Despair 's a dreadful thing,
And does poor mortals bring
Unto the bitter sting
  Of death and hell.

Sweet wife and heart's delight !
I had been ruined quite
In death's eternal night,
  Hadst thou not been
The happy instrument
That ruin to prevent ;
Love, joy, and sweet content,
  I now am in.

Tho' slender is my store,
Yet I'll despair no more ;
That man is truly poor,
  Who wants content ;
But where content 's increased,
'Tis a continual feast,
Praise God, I am released,
  Death to prevent.

As God gives me grace,
This council I'll embrace ;
Despair shall not take place
  In me henceforth ;

Farewell, litigious strife;
And come, my cheerful wife,
Thy words have saved my life,
   God bless us both,

And all mankind likewise,
From the calamities,
Which do as fogs arise,
   From foul despair ;
Let doubtful Christians fly,
In their extremity,
To God who sits on high,
   By fervent prayer.

He is a man's friend in chief,
The fountain of relief:
When I was lost in grief,
   And at the worst,
My dear indulgent bride,
Her council was my guide ;
In God I'm satisfied,
   In whom I trust.

My children, wife, and I,
We will ourselves apply
To true industry,
   And leave the rest
To Providence divine ;
Henceforth I'll not repine,
I hope that me and mine
   Shall still be blest.

Thus, by the good wife's care,
The husband in despair
Was brought at length to bear
   His sorrows rife;
The bitter cup of grief,
Her words did yield relief,
She was his friend in chief,
   And faithful wife.

Good men and women, pray,
That hear me now this day,
Labour now without delay,
   To live in love:
Assist each other still,
In fortune good or ill,
Then you'll have a blessing still,
   Come from above.

———

VIII.

𝔖𝔪𝔬𝔨𝔦𝔫𝔤 𝔖𝔭𝔦𝔯𝔦𝔱𝔲𝔞𝔩𝔦𝔷𝔢𝔡.

By Ralph Erskine, V.D.M.

THE Rev. Ralph Erskine, or, as he chose to designate himself,
"Ralph Erskine, V.D.M.," the pious author of "Smoking Spiritualized," was born at Monilaws, in the county of Northumberland,
on the 15th of March 1685. He was brother to the Rev.
Ebenezer Erskine, minister of the gospel at Stirling, and son of
the Rev. Henry Erskine, who was one of the thirty-three children
of Ralph Erskine of Shieldfield; a family of considerable repute,

and originally descended from the ancient house of Marr. He was educated at the College in Edinburgh, and obtained his license to preach from the Presbytery of Dunfermline on the 8th of June, 1709. Receiving an unanimous invitation from the Church at Dunfermline in May 1711, he accepted the call, and was ordained over them in August the same year. In July 1714, he married Margaret Dewar, the daughter of the Laird of Lassodie, by whom he had five sons, and five daughters, all of whom died in the prime of life. In 1732, he married Margaret, daughter of Mr. Simson of Edinburgh, by whom he had four sons, one of whom, with his wife, survived him. He published a great number of sermons,—*A Paraphrase on the Canticles*,—a volume entitled *Scripture Songs*, a *Treatise on Mental Images, or Faith no Fancy;* but his *Gospel Sonnets* were not published till after his decease. On the 29th October 1752, he was seized with a nervous fever, which terminated his life on the 6th of November, after an illness of only eight days, in the sixty-eighth year of his age.

The *Smoking Spiritualized* is, at the present day, a standard publication with our modern ballad-printers, but their copies are one and all exceedingly corrupt. Erskine no doubt wrote this curious poem as an antidote to a class of broadsides at one time very common, and still to be found in country inns, in which scripture is profanely paraphrased, and made to encourage tippling; such as—

> " Give him strong drink
> Until he wink,
>   That's sinking in despair."

Of this latter description of publications the editor could have given several specimens, but their profanity induces him to withhold them. They are very witty and quaint, and that is their *only* recommendation.

PART I.

THIS Indian weed, now withered quite,
Though green at noon, cut down at night,
   Shows thy decay ;
   All flesh is hay :
      Thus think, and smoke tobacco.

The pipe so lily-like and weak,
Does thus thy mortal state bespeak ;
    Thou art e'en such,—
    Gone with a touch.
        Thus think, and smoke tobacco.

And when the smoke ascends on high,
Then thou beholdst the vanity
    Of worldly stuff,
    Gone with a puff.
        Thus think, and smoke tobacco.

And when the pipe grows foul within,
Think on thy soul defiled with sin ;
    For then the fire
    It does require :
        Thus think, and smoke tobacco.

And seest the ashes cast away,
Then to thyself thou mayest say,
    That to the dust
    Return thou must.
        Thus think, and smoke tobacco.

PART II.

Was this small plant for thee cut down ?
So was the plant of great renown,
    Which Mercy sends
    For nobler ends.
        Thus think, and smoke tobacco.

Doth juice medicinal proceed
From such a naughty foreign weed?
    Then what's the power
    Of Jesse's flower?
        Thus think, and smoke tobacco.

The promise, like the pipe, inlays,
And by the mouth of faith conveys,
    What virtue flows
    From Sharon's rose.
        Thus think, and smoke tobacco.

In vain the unlighted pipe you blow,
Your pains in outward means are so,
    'Till heavenly fire
    Your heart inspire.
        Thus think, and smoke tobacco.

The smoke, like burning incense, towers,
So should a praying heart of yours,
    With ardent cries,
    Surmount the skies.
        Thus think, and smoke tobacco.

IX.

The Masonic Hymn.

THIS is a very ancient production, though given from a modern
copy; it has always been popular amongst the poor " brethren of
the mystic tie." The late Henry O'Brien, A.B., quotes the

seventh verse in his essay *On the Round Towers of Ireland.* He generally had a common copy of the hymn in his pocket, and on meeting with any of his antiquarian friends who were not Masons, was in the habit of thrusting it into their hands, and telling them that if they understood the mystical allusions it contained, they would be in possession of a key which would unlock the pyramids of Egypt! The tune to the hymn is peculiar to it, and is of a plaintive and solemn character.

COME all you freemasons that dwell around the globe,
That wear the badge of innocence, I mean the royal
      robe,
Which Noah he did wear when in the ark he stood,
When the world was destroyed by a deluging flood.

Noah he was virtuous in the sight of the Lord,
He loved a freemason that kept the secret word;
For he built the ark, and he planted the first vine,
Now his soul in heaven like an angel doth shine.

Once I was blind, and could not see the light,
Then up to Jerusalem I took my flight,
I was led by the evangelist through a wilderness of care,
You may see by the sign and the badge that I wear.

On the 13th rose the ark, let us join hand in hand,
For the Lord spake to Moses by water and by land,
Unto the pleasant river where by Eden it did rin,
And Eve tempted Adam by the serpent of sin.

When I think of Moses it makes me to blush,
All on mount Horeb where I saw the burning bush;
My shoes I'll throw off, and my staff I'll cast away,
And I'll wander like a pilgrim unto my dying day.

When I think of Aaron it makes me to weep,   [feet;
Likewise of the Virgin Mary who lay at our Saviour's
'Twas in the garden of Gethsemane where he had the
          bloody sweat ;
Repent, my dearest brethren, before it is too late.

I thought I saw twelve dazzling lights, which put me
          in surprise,
And gazing all around me I heard a dismal noise ;
The serpent passed by me which fell unto the ground,
With great joy and comfort the secret word I found.

Some say it is lost, but surely it is found,
And so is our Saviour, it is known to all around ;
Search all the scriptures over and there it will be shewn
The tree that will bear no fruit must be cut down.

Abraham was a man well beloved by the Lord,
He was true to be found in great Jehovah's word,
He stretched forth his hand, and took a knife to slay
          his son,
An angel appearing said, the Lord's will be done.

O, Abraham ! O, Abraham ! lay no hand upon the lad,
He sent him unto thee to make thy heart glad ;
Thy seed shall increase like stars in the sky,
And thy soul into heaven like Gabriel shall fly.

O, never, O, never will I hear an orphan cry,
Nor yet a gentle virgin until the day I die ;

You wandering Jews that travel the wide world round,
May knock at the door where truth is to be found.

Often against the Turks and Infidels we fight,
To let the wandering world know we're in the right,
For in heaven there's a lodge, and St. Peter keeps the
              door,
And none can enter in but those that are pure.

St. Peter he opened, and so we entered in,
Into the holy seat secure, which is all free from sin ;
St. Peter he opened, and so we entered there,
And the glory of the temple no man can compare.

X.

A Dialogue between the Husband=man and the Serving=man.

This ancient dialogue has long been used at country merry-
makings. The editor was present in 1835 at an harvest-home
feast at Selborne, in Hampshire, when he heard the dialogue
recited by two country-men, who gave it with considerable
humour, and dramatic effect. It is said in a sort of chant, or
recitative. Davies Gilbert published a copy in his *Ancient
Christmas Carols*. The editor has several printed copies, but all
of modern date. The following version is a traditional one
from Sussex, which has been collated with another traditional
one communicated by W. Sandys, Esq., F.S.A. In the modern
editions the term "servant-man" has been substituted for the
more ancient designation.

SERVING-MAN.

WELL met, my brother friend, all at this highway end,
  So simple all alone, as you can,
I pray you tell to me, what may your calling be,
  Are you not a serving-man?

HUSBAND-MAN.

No, no, my brother dear, what makes you to enquire
  Of any such a thing at my hand?
Indeed I shall not feign, but I will tell you plain,
  I am a downright husband-man.

SERVING-MAN.

If a husband-man you be, then go along with me,
  And quickly you shall see out of hand,
How in a little space I will help you to a place,
  Where you may be a serving-man.

HUSBAND-MAN.

Kind sir! I 'turn you thanks for your intelligence,
  These things I receive at your hand;
But something pray now show, that first I may plainly
    know
  The pleasures of a serving-man.

SERVING-MAN.

Why a serving-man has pleasure beyond all sort of
    measure,
  With his hawk on his fist, as he does stand;

For the game that he does kill, and the meat that does
    him fill,
    Are pleasures for the serving-man.

HUSBAND-MAN.

And my pleasure 's more than that, to see my oxen fat,
    And a good stock of hay by them stand ;
My plowing and my sowing, my reaping and my mowing,
    Are pleasures for the husband-man.

SERVING-MAN.

Why it is a gallant thing to ride out with a king,
    With a lord, duke, or any such man ;
To hear the horns to blow, and see the hounds all
    in a row,
    That is pleasure for the serving-man.

HUSBAND-MAN.

But my pleasure's more I know, to see my corn to grow,
    So thriving all over my land ;
And, therefore, I do mean, with my ploughing with my
    team,
    To keep myself a husband-man.

SERVING-MAN.

Why the diet that we eat is the choicest of all meat,
    Such as pig, goose, capon, and swan ;
Our pastry is so fine, we drink sugar in our wine,
    That is living for the serving-man.

HUSBAND-MAN.

Talk not of goose nor capon, give me good beef or
      bacon,
  And good bread and cheese, now at hand ;
With pudding, brawn, and souse, all in a farmer's
      house,
  That is living for the husband-man.

SERVING-MAN.

Why the clothing that we wear is delicate and rare,
  With our coat, lace, buckles, and band ;
Our shirts are white as milk, and our stockings they are
      silk,
  That is clothing for a serving-man.

HUSBAND-MAN.

But I value not a hair your delicate fine wear,
  Such as gold is laced upon ;
Give me a good grey coat, and in my purse a groat,
  That is clothing for the husband-man.

SERVING-MAN.

Kind sir ! it would be bad if none could be had
  Those tables for to wait upon ;
There is no lord, duke, nor squire, nor member for the
      shire,
  Can do without a serving-man.

HUSBAND-MAN.

But, Jack ! it would be worse if there was none of us
  To follow the ploughing of the land;

There is neither king, lord, nor squire, nor member for
     the shire,
  Can do without the husband-man.

SERVING-MAN.

Kind sir! I must confess 't, and I humbly protest
  I will give you the uppermost hand,
Although your labour 's painful, and mine it is so very
     gainful,
  I wish I were a husband-man.

HUSBAND-MAN.

So come now, let us all, both great as well as small,
  Pray for the grain of our land;
And let us, whatsoever, do all our best endeavour,
  For to maintain the good husband-man.

XI.

Lydford Law.

By William Browne, author of *Britannia's Pastorals.*

THE peasants of Devonshire repeat portions of the following
witty poem as they have been traditionally handed down, but are
ignorant of the source from whence they are derived. The poem
was first printed in Prince's *Worthies of Devon,* 1701. William
Browne, the author, was born at Tavistock, in 1590. In the
Anglo-Saxon times, the town of Lidford on Dartmoor, had the
privilege of coining, and long after such privilege was abolished,
courts were held there for the purpose of trying all offences connected with coining, as well as for the settling of mining disputes.
It is almost unnecessary to remind the reader that by the old
law of the land, the offence of coining was considered treason,
and criminals convicted thereof, were subjected to all the disgust-
ing punishments which, till a very recent period, were inflicted

on actual traitors. Some interesting particulars respecting
Lidford and its judges, one of whom was the notorious Jefferies,
may be found in Mrs. Bray's *Traditions of Devonshire*, London
1826.

I OFT have heard of Lydford law,
How in the morn they hang and draw,
 And sit in judgment after:
At first I wondered at it much;
But since I find the reason such,
 As it deserves no laughter.

They have a castle on a hill,
I took it for an old wind-mill,
 The vanes blown off by weather:
To lye therein one night 'tis guessed,
'Twere better to be stoned and pressed,
 Or hanged; now chose you whether.

Ten men less room within this cave,
Than five mice in a lanthorn have,
 The keepers they are sly ones;
If any could devise by art
To get it up into a cart,
 'Twere fit to carry lyons.

When I beheld it, Lord! thought I,
What justice and what clemency
 Hath Lydford, when I saw all!
I know none gladly there would stay;
But rather hang out of the way,
 Then tarry for a tryal.

The prince an hundred pound hath sent,
To mend the leads and planchens wrent,
   Within this living tomb;
Some forty-five pounds more had paid,
The debts of all that shall be laid
   There till the day of doom.

One lyes there for a seam of malt;
Another for a peck of salt;
   Two sureties for a noble.
If this be true, or else false news,
You may go ask of master Crews,*
   John Vaughan, or John Doble.†

* The steward of the court.
† Attorneys of the court.

More, to these men that lye in lurch,
There is a bridge, there is a church,
   Seven ashes, and one oak:
Three houses standing, and ten down;
They say the parson hath a gown,
   But I saw ne'er a cloak.

Whereby you may consider well,
That plain simplicity doth dwell
   At Lydford, without bravery:
And in the town, both young and grave
Do love the naked truth to have;
   No cloak to hide their knavery.

The people all within this clime
Are frozen in the winter-time,
　For sure I do not fain:
And when the summer is begun,
They lye like silk-worms in the sun,
　And come to life again.

One told me in King Cæsar's time,
The town was built with stone and lime;
　But sure the walls were clay:
And they are fallen for aught I see;
And since the houses are got free,
　The town is run away.

Oh! Cæsar, if thou there didst reign,
While our house stands come there again,
　Come quickly while there is one;
If thou stay but a little fit,
But five years more, they will commit
　The whole town to a prison.

To see it thus, much grieved was I:
The proverb saith, sorrows be dry;
　So was I at the matter;
Now by good luck, I know not how,
There thither came a strange stray cow,
　And we had milk and water.

To nine good stomachs with our whigg,
At last we got a roasting pigg;

E

This dyet was our bounds;
And this was just as if 'twere known,
A pound of butter had been thrown
    Among a pack of hounds.

One glass of drink I got by chance,
'Twas claret when it was in France;
    But now from it much wider:
I think a man might make as good
With green crabs boyled, and Brazil wood,
    And half a pint of cyder.

I kissed the mayor's hand of the town,
Who, though he wears no scarlet gown,
    Honours the rose and thistle:
A piece of coral to the mace,
Which there I saw to serve in place,
    Would make a good child's whistle.

At six a clock I came away,
And prayed for those that were to stay
    Within a place so arrant:
Wide and ope, the winds so roar,
By God's grace I'll come there no more,
    Unless by some Tyn Warrant.

XII.

Description of St. Keyne's Well,

CORNWALL.

THE following lines are to be found in Carew's *Survey of Cornwall*, 1602, but are probably much older than that date. They are frequently recited by the peasantry of Cornwall, especially by those who reside near the famous "Well of Saint Keyne," the sacred spring concerning which a very excellent and humorous ballad was written by the poet Southey.

———

IN name, in shape, in quality,
    This well is very quaint,
The name to lot of Kayne befell,
    No over-holy saint.

The shape four trees of divers kinde,
    Withy, Oke, Elme and Ash,
Make with their roots an archèd roofe,
    Whose floore this spring doth wash.

The quality, that man or wife,
    Whose chance, or choice attaines,
First of this sacred streame to drinke,
    Thereby the mastry gaines.

———

ANCIENT POEMS, BALLADS, &c.

BALLADS.

I.

𝕶𝖎𝖓𝖌 𝕳𝖊𝖓𝖗𝖎𝖊 𝖙𝖍𝖊 𝕱𝖎𝖋𝖙𝖍'𝖘 𝕮𝖔𝖓𝖖𝖚𝖊𝖘𝖙.

(TRADITIONAL VERSION.)

A BALLAD on the same subject as the following one is to be found in the *Crown-Garland of Golden Roses*, Part II., 1659. Vide Percy Society's edit. p. 65, entitled *The Battel of Agincourt betweene the Englishmen and the Frenchmen*, but it is totally different from *King Henry the Fifth's Conquest*, which the editor took down from the singing of the late Francis King, of Skipton in Craven, an eccentric character, who was well known in the western dales of Yorkshire as "the Skipton Minstrel." King's version does not contain the third verse, which is obtained, as is also the title, from a modern broadside, from whence, also, one or two verbal corrections are made, of too trifling a nature to particularize. The tune to which King used to sing it, is the same as that of *The Bold Pedlar and Robin Hood.* The ballad is old, and can be traced to the sixteenth century. It is evidently the ballad alluded to in *An excellent Medley, to the tune of Tarleton's Medley,* and which is to be found in the Roxburgh Collection, "Originally printed for Henry Gosson, and afterwards by F. Coles, T. Vere, and S. Wright." Gosson was living is 1609. The line quoted in the *Medley*, though given incorrectly for the sake of a rhyme, appears to be the first line of the thirteenth verse.

The story of the Tennis-balls is not the mere invention of a ballad-monger, but is recorded by some grave historians. "It is reported," says Hume, "by some historians, (see *Hist. Croyl. Cont.*, p. 500), that the Dauphin, in derision of Henry's claims and dissolute character, sent him a box of tennis-balls, intimating that these implements of play were better adapted to him than

the instruments of war. But this story is by no means credible:
the great offers made by the court of France, show that they had
already entertained a just idea of Henry's character, as well as
of their own situation." — Vide *Hume's History of England*,
Chap. XIX.

————

As our King lay musing on his bed,
He bethought himself upon a time,
Of a tribute that was due from France,
Had not been paid for so long a time.

>   Down, a down, a down, a down,
>   Down, a down, a down.

He callèd on his trusty page,
His trusty page then callèd he,
Oh you must go to the King of France,
Oh you must go right speedilie.

>   Down, a down, &c.

And tell him of my tribute due,
Ten ton of gold that's due to me ;
That he must send me my tribute home,
Or in French land he soon will me see.

>   Down, a down, &c.

Oh ! then away went the trusty page,
Away, away, and away went he,
Until he came to the King of France,
Lo ! he fell down on his bended knee.

>   Down, a down, &c.

My master greets you, worthy Sire,
Ten ton of gold there is due, says he ;
You must send him his tribute home,
Or in French land you will soon him see.
   Down, a down, &c.

Your master 's young, and of tender years,
Not fit to come into my degree ;
But I will send him three tennis balls,
That with them learn to play may he.
   Down, a down, &c.

Oh then away came the trusty page,
Away, away, and away came he,
Until he came to our gracious King,
Lo ! he fell down on his bended knee.
   Down, a down, &c.

What news, what news, my trusty page,
What news, what news hast thou brought to me?
I've brought such news from the King of France,
That you and he will ne'er agree.
   Down, a down, &c.

He says you're young, and of tender years,
Not fit to come into his degree,
But he will send you three tennis balls,
That with them you may learn to play.
   Down, a down, &c.

Oh! then bespoke our noble King,
A solemn vow then vowèd he,
I'll promise him such tennis balls,
As in French lands he ne'er did see.
　　　Down, a down, &c.

Go, call up Cheshire and Lancashìre,
And Derby hills, that are so free;
Not a married man, nor a widow's son,
For the widow's cry shall not go with me.
　　　Down, a down, &c.

They called up Cheshire and Lancashìre,
And Derby lads that were so free,
Not a married man nor a widow's son,
Yet they were a jovial bold companie.
　　　Down, a down, &c.

Oh! then he sailed to fair French land,
With drums and trumpets so merrilie,
Oh! then bespoke the King of France,
Yonder comes proud King Henrie.
　　　Down, a down, &c.

The first fire that the Frenchmen gave,
They killed our Englishmen so free,
We killed ten thousand of the French,
And the rest of them they were forced to flee.
　　　Down, a down, &c.

And then we marched to Paris gates,
With drums and trumpets so merrilie;
Oh! then bespoke the King of France,
Lord! have mercy on my poor men and me!
        Down, a down, &c.

Go! tell him I'll send home his tribute due,
Ten ton of gold that is due from me;
And the fairest flower that is in our French land
To the Rose of England it shall go free.
        Down, a down, &c.

II.

The Three Knights.

(TRADITIONAL.)

The Three Knights was first printed by the late Davies Gilbert,
F.R.S., in the appendix to his work on *Christmas Carols.* Mr.
Gilbert thought that some verses were wanting after the eighth
stanza; the present editor is of a different opinion. A conjectural emendation made in the ninth verse, viz., the substitution
of *far* for *for*, seems to render the ballad perfect. The ballad is
still popular amongst the peasantry in the West of England.
The tune is given by Gilbert.

THERE did three Knights come from the west,
    With the high and the lily oh!
And these three Knights courted one Ladye,
    As the rose was so sweetly blown.

The first Knight came was all in white,
   With the high and the lily oh !
And asked of her if she'd be his delight,
   As the rose was so sweetly blown.

The next Knight came was all in green,
   With the high and the lily oh !
And asked of her, if she'd be his Queen,
   As the rose was so sweetly blown.

The third Knight came was all in red,
   With the high and the lily oh !
And asked of her, if she would wed,
   As the rose was so sweetly blown.

Then have you asked of my father dear ?
   With the high and the lily oh !
Likewise of her who did me bear ?
   As the rose was so sweetly blown.

And have you asked of my brother John ?
   With the high and the lily oh !
And also of my sister Anne ?
   As the rose was so sweetly blown.

Yes, I've asked of your father dear,
   With the high and the lily oh !
Likewise of her who did you bear,
   As the rose was so sweetly blown.

And I've asked of your sister Anne,
  With the high and the lily oh !
But I've not asked of your brother John,
  As the rose was so sweetly blown.

Far on the road as they rode along,
  With the high and the lily oh!
There did they meet with her brother John,
  As the rose was so sweetly blown.

She stoopèd low to kiss him sweet,
  With the high and the lily oh!
He to her heart did a dagger meet,
  As the rose was so sweetly blown.

Ride on, ride on, cried the serving man,
  With the high and the lily oh!
Methinks your bride she looks wondrous wan,
  As the rose was so sweetly blown.

I wish I were on yonder stile,
  With the high and the lily oh!
For there I would sit and bleed awhile,
  As the rose was so sweetly blown.

I wish I were on yonder hill,
  With the high and the lily oh!
There I'd alight and make my will,
  As the rose was so sweetly blown.

What would you give to your father dear?
　　With the high and the lily oh!
The gallant steed which doth me bear,
　　As the rose was so sweetly blown.

What would you give to your mother dear?
　　With the high and the lily oh!
My wedding shift which I do wear,
　　As the rose was so sweetly blown.

But she must wash it very clean,
　　With the high and the lily oh!
For my heart's blood sticks in every seam,
　　As the rose was so sweetly blown.

What would you give to your sister Anne?
　　With the high and the lily oh!
My gay gold ring, and my featherèd fan,
　　As the rose was so sweetly blown.

What would you give to your brother John?
　　With the high and the lily oh!
A rope and a gallows to hang him on,
　　As the rose was so sweetly blown.

What would you give to your brother John's wife?
　　With the high and the lily oh!
A widow's weeds, and a quiet life,
　　As the rose was so sweetly blown.

III.

𝕿𝖍𝖊 𝕭𝖑𝖎𝖓𝖉 𝕭𝖊𝖌𝖌𝖆𝖗 𝖔𝖋 𝕭𝖊𝖉𝖓𝖆𝖑𝖑 𝕲𝖗𝖊𝖊𝖓.

SHEWING HOW HIS DAUGHTER WAS MARRIED TO A KNIGHT,
AND HAD THREE THOUSAND POUND TO
HER PORTION.

PERCY'S copy of *The Beggar's Daughter of Bednall Green* is known
to be very incorrect: besides many alterations and improvements
which it received at the hands of the Bishop, it contains no less
than eight stanzas written by Robert Dodsley, the author of *The
Economy of Human Life*.   So far as poetry is concerned, there
cannot be a question that the version in the *Reliques* is far superior to the original, which is still a popular favourite, and a
correct copy of which is now given, as it has existed in all the
common broadside editions that have appeared from 1672 to the
present time.   Although the original copies have all perished,
the ballad has been very satisfactorily proved by Percy to have
been written in the reign of Elizabeth.   The present reprint is
from a modern copy, carefully collated with one in the Bagford
Collection, entitled,

> " The rarest ballad that ever was seen,
>   Of the Blind Beggar's Daughter of Bednal Green."

The imprint to it is, " Printed by and for W. Onley ; and are
to be sold by C. Bates, at the sign of the Sun and Bible, in Pye
Corner."   The very antiquated orthography adopted in some
editions of *The Blind Beggar*, does not rest on any authority.

PART I.

THIS song 's of a beggar who long lost his sight,
And had a fair daughter, most pleasant and bright,
And many a gallant brave suitor had she,
And none was so comely as pretty Bessee.

And though she was of complexion most fair,
And seeing she was but a beggar his heir,
Of ancient housekeepers despisèd was she,
Whose sons came as suitors to pretty Bessee.

Wherefore in great sorrow fair Bessee did say:
Good father and mother, let me now go away,
To seek out my fortune, whatever it be.
This suit then was granted to pretty Bessee.

This Bessee, that was of a beauty most bright,
They clad in gray russet, and late in the night
From father and mother alone parted she,
Who sighèd and sobbèd for pretty Bessee.

She went till she came to Stratford-at-Bow,
Then she knew not whither or which way to go,
With tears she lamented her sad destiny;
So sad and so heavy was pretty Bessee.

She kept on her journey until it was day,
And went unto Rumford, along the highway;
And at the Kings Arms entertainèd was she,
So fair and well favoured was pretty Bessee.

She had not been there one month at an end,
But master and mistress and all was her friend:
And every brave gallant that once did her see,
Was straightway in love with pretty Bessee.

Great gifts they did send her of silver and gold,
And in their songs daily her love they extoll'd:
Her beauty was blazèd in every degree,
So fair and so comely was pretty Bessee.

The young men of Rumford in her had their joy,
She shewed herself courteous, but never too coy,
And at their commandment still she would be,
So fair and so comely was pretty Bessee.

Four suitors at once unto her did go,
They cravèd her favour, but still she said no;
I would not have gentlemen marry with me!
Yet ever they honourèd pretty Bessee.

Now one of them was a gallant young knight,
And he came unto her disguised in the night;
The second, a gentleman of high degree,
Who wooèd and suèd for pretty Bessee.

A merchant of London, whose wealth was not small,
Was then the third suitor, and proper withal;
Her master's own son the fourth man must be,
Who swore he would die for pretty Bessee.

If that thou wilt marry with me, quoth the knight,
I'll make thee a lady with joy and delight;
My heart is enthrallèd in thy fair beauty,
Then grant me thy favour, my pretty Bessee.

The gentleman said, Come marry with me,
In silks and in velvet my Bessee shall be;
My heart lies distracted, oh! hear me, quoth he,
And grant me thy love, my dear pretty Bessee.

Let me be thy husband, the merchant did say,
Thou shalt live in London most gallant and gay;
My ships shall bring home rich jewels for thee,
And I will for ever love pretty Bessee.

Then Bessee she sighèd and thus she did say;
My father and mother I mean to obey;
First get their good will, and be faithful to me,
And you shall enjoy your dear pretty Bessee.

To every one of them that answer she made,
Therefore unto her they joyfully said:
This thing to fulfill we all now agree,
But where dwells thy father, my pretty Bessee?

My father, quoth she, is soon to be seen:
The silly blind beggar of Bednall Green,
That daily sits begging for charity,
He is the kind father of pretty Bessee.

His marks and his token are knowen full well,
He always is led by a dog and a bell;
A poor silly old man, God knoweth, is he,
Yet he is the true father of pretty Bessee.

Nay, nay, quoth the merchant, thou art not for me;
She, quoth the inn holder, my wife shall not be;
I loathe, said the gentleman, a beggars degree,
Therefore, now farewell, my pretty Bessee.

Why then, quoth the knight, happ better or worse,
I weigh not true love by the weight of the purse,
And beauty is beauty in every degree,
Then welcome to me, my dear pretty Bessee.

With thee to thy father forthwith I will go.
Nay, forbear, quoth his kinsman, it must not be so:
A poor beggars daughter a lady shan't be;
Then take thy adieu of thy pretty Bessee.

As soon then as it was break of the day,
The knight had from Rumford stole Bessee away;
The young men of Rumford, so sick as may be,
Rode after to fetch again pretty Bessee.

As swift as the wind to ride they were seen,
Until they came near unto Bednall Green,
And as the knight lighted most courteously,
They fought against him for pretty Bessee.

But rescue came presently over the plain,
Or else the knight there for his love had been slain;
The fray being ended, they straightway did see
His kinsman come railing at pretty Bessee.

Then bespoke the blind beggar, altho' I be poor,
Rail not against my child at my own door,
Though she be not deckèd in velvet and pearl,
Yet I will drop angels with thee for my girl;

And then if my gold should better her birth,
And equal the gold you lay on the earth,
Then neither rail you, nor grudge you to see
The blind beggars daughter a lady to be.

But first, I will hear, and have it well known,
The gold that you drop it shall be all your own;
With that they replièd, Contented we be;
Then heres, quoth the beggar, for pretty Bessee.

With that an angel he dropped on the ground,
And droppèd, in angels, full three thousand pound;
And oftentimes it provèd most plain,
For the gentlemans one, the beggar dropped twain.

So that the whole place wherein they did sit,
With gold was coverèd every whit;
The gentleman having dropt all his store,
Said, Beggar! your hand hold, for I have no more.

Thou hast fulfillèd thy promise aright,
Then marry my girl, quoth he, to the knight;
And then, quoth he, I will throw you down,
An hundred pound more to buy her a gown.

F

The gentlemen all, who his treasure had seen,
Admirèd the beggar of Bednall Green;
And those that had been her suitors before,
Their tender flesh for anger they tore.

Thus was the fair Bessee matched to a knight,
And made a lady in others despite.
A fairer lady there never was seen
Than the blind beggars daughter of Bednall Green.

But of her sumptuous marriage and feast,
And what fine lords and ladies there prest,
The second part shall set forth to your sight,
With marvellous pleasure, and wished for delight.

Of a blind beggar's daughter so bright,
That late was betrothed to a young knight,
All the whole discourse therefore you may see,
But now comes the wedding of pretty Bessee.

————

PART II.

IT was in a gallant palace most brave,
Adornèd with all the cost they could have,
This wedding it was kept most sumptuously,
And all for the love of pretty Bessee.

And all kind of dainties and delicates sweet,
Was brought to their banquet, as it was thought meet,
Partridge, and plover, and venison most free,
Against the brave wedding of pretty Bessee.

The wedding thro' England was spread by report,
So that a great number thereto did resort,
Of nobles and gentles of every degree,
And all for the fame of pretty Bessee.

To church then away went this gallant young knight,
His bride followed after, an angel most bright,
With troops of ladies, the like was ne'er seen,
As went with sweet Bessee of Bednall Green.

This wedding being solemnized then,
With music performèd by skilfullest men,
The nobles and gentlemen down at the side,
Each one beholding the beautiful bride.

But after the sumptuous dinner was done,
To talk and to reason a number begun,
And of the blind beggars daughter most bright;
And what with his daughter he gave to the knight.

Then spoke the nobles, Much marvel have we
This jolly blind beggar we cannot yet see!
My lords, quoth the bride, my father so base
Is loath with his presence these states to disgrace.

The praise of a woman in question to bring,
Before her own face is a flattering thing;
But we think thy fathers baseness, quoth they,
Might by thy beauty be clean put away.

They no sooner this pleasant word spoke,
But in comes the beggar in a silken cloak,
A velvet cap and a feather had he,
And now a musician, forsooth, he would be.

And being led in from catching of harm,
He had a dainty lute under his arm,
Said, please you to hear any music of me,
A song I will give you of pretty Bessee.

With that his lute he twangèd straightway,
And thereon began most sweetly to play,
And after a lesson was played two or three,
He strained out this song most delicately:—

A BEGGAR's daughter did dwell on a green,
Who for her beauty may well be a queen,
A blithe bonny lass, and dainty was she,
And many one callèd her pretty Bessee.

Her father he had no goods nor no lands,
But begged for a penny all day with his hands,
And yet for her marriage gave thousands three,
Yet still he hath somewhat for pretty Bessee.

And here if any one do her disdain,
Her father is ready with might and with main
To prove she is come of noble degree,
Therefore let none flout at my pretty Bessee.

With that the lords and the company round
With a hearty laughter were ready to swound;
At last said the lords, Full well we may see,
The bride and the bridegrooms beholden to thee.

With that the fair bride all blushing did rise,
With chrystal water all in her bright eyes,
Pardon my father, brave nobles, quoth she,
That through blind affection thus doats upon me.

If this be thy father, the nobles did say,
Well may he be proud of this happy day,
Yet by his countenance well may we see,
His birth with his fortune could never agree;

And therefore, blind beggar, we pray thee bewray,
And look to us then the truth thou dost say,
Thy birth and thy parentage what it may be,
E'en for the love thou bearest to pretty Bessee.

Then give me leave, ye gentles each one,
A song more to sing and then I'll begone,
And if that I do not win good report,
Then do not give me one groat for my sport:—

WHEN first our king his fame did advance,
And sought his title in delicate France,
In many places great perils past he,
But then was not born my pretty Bessee.

And at those wars went over to fight,
Many a brave duke, a lord, and a knight,
And with them young Monford of courage so free,
But then was not born my pretty Bessee.

And there did young Monford with a blow on the face
Lose both his eyes in a very short space;
His life had been gone away with his sight,
Had not a young woman gone forth in the night.

Among the said men, her fancy did move,
To search and to seek for her own true love,
Who seeing young Monford there gasping to die,
She savèd his life through her charity.

And then all our victuals in beggars attire,
At the hands of good people we then did require,
At last into England, as now it is seen,
We came, and remainèd in Bednall Green.

And thus we have livèd in Fortune's despyght,
Though poor, yet contented with humble delight,
And in my old years, a comfort to me,
God sent me a daughter called pretty Bessee.

And thus, ye nobles, my song I do end,
Hoping by the same no man to offend;
Full forty long winters thus I have been,
A silly blind beggar of Bednall Green.

Now when the company every one,
Did hear the strange tale he told in his song,
They were amazèd, as well they might be
Both at the blind beggar and pretty Bessee.

With that the fair bride they all did embrace,
Saying, You are come of an honourable race,
Thy father likewise is of high degree,
And thou art right worthy a lady to be.

Thus was the feast ended with joy and delight,
A happy bridegroom was made the young knight,
Who livèd in great joy and felicity,
With his fair lady dear pretty Bessee.

IV.

The Bold Pedlar and Robin Hood.

THIS ballad is of considerable antiquity, and no doubt much
older than some of those inserted in the common garlands. It
appears to have escaped the notice of Ritson, Percy, and other
collectors of Robin Hood ballads. An aged female in Bermond-
sey, Surrey, from whose oral recitation the editor took down the
present version, informed him that she had often heard her
grandmother sing it, and that it was never in print; but he has
of late met with several common stall copies.

THERE chanced to be a pedlar bold,
    A pedlar bold he chanced to be;
He rolled his pack all on his back,
    And he came tripping o'er the lee.
        Down, a down, a down, a down,
        Down, a down, a down.

By chance he met two troublesome blades,
   Two troublesome blades they chanced to be;
The one of them was bold Robin Hood,
   And the other was little John, so free.

Oh! pedlar, pedlar, what is in thy pack,
   Come speedilie and tell to me?
I've several suits of the gay green silks,
   And silken bow strings two or three.

If you have several suits of the gay green silk,
   And silken bow strings two or three,
Then it's by my body, cries little John,
   One half your pack shall belong to me.

Oh! nay, oh! nay, says the pedlar bold,
   Oh! nay, oh! nay, that never can be,
For there's never a man from fair Nottingham
   Can take one half my pack from me.

Then the pedlar he pulled off his pack,
   And put it a little below his knee,
Saying, If you do move me one perch from this,
   My pack and all shall gang with thee.

Then little John he drew his sword;
   The pedlar by his pack did stand;
They fought until they both did sweat,
   Till he cried, Pedlar, pray hold your hand!

Then Robin Hood he was standing by,
　　And he did laugh most heartilie,
Saying, I could find a man of a smaller scale,
　　Could thrash the pedlar, and also thee.

Go, you try, master, says little John,
　　Go, you try, master, most speedilie,
Or by my body, says little John,
　　I am sure this night you will not know me.

Then Robin Hood he drew his sword,
　　And the pedlar by his pack did stand,
They fought till the blood in streams did flow,
　　Till he cried, Pedlar, pray hold your hand!

Pedlar, pedlar! what is thy name?
　　Come speedilie and tell to me;
My name! my name, I ne'er will tell,
　　Till both your names you have told to me.

The one of us is bold Robin Hood,
　　And the other little John, so free:
Now, says the pedlar, it lays to my good will,
　　Whether my name I chuse to tell to thee.

I am Gamble Gold of the gay green woods,
　　And travelled far beyond the sea;
For killing a man in my father's land,
　　From my country I was forced to flee.

If you are Gamble Gold of the gay green woods,
    And travelled far beyond the sea,
You are my mother's own sister's son;
    What nearer cousins then can we be?

They sheathed their swords with friendly words,
    So merrily they did agree,
They went to a tavern and there they dined,
    And bottles cracked most merrilie.

---

v.

The Outlandish Knight.

THIS is the common English stall copy of a ballad of which
there are a variety of versions, for an account of which, and of
the presumed origin of the story, the reader is referred to the
notes on the *Water o' Wearie's Well*, in the editor's *Scottish Traditional Versions of Ancient Ballads*, Percy Society's publications,
No. LVIII. By the term "outlandish" is signified an inhabitant
of that portion of the border which was formerly known by the
name of "the Debateable Land," a district which, though
claimed by both England and Scotland, could not be said to
belong to either country. The people on each side of the border applied the term "outlandish" to the Debateable residents.
The tune to *The Outlandish Knight* has never been printed; it is
peculiar to the ballad, and, from its popularity, is well known.

AN Outlandish knight came from the North lands,
    And he came a wooing to me;
He told me he'd take me unto the North lands,
    And there he would marry me.

Come, fetch me some of your father's gold,
    And some of your mother's fee ;
And two of the best nags out of the stable,
    Where they stand thirty and three.

She fetched him some of her father's gold,
    And some of the mother's fee ;
And two of the best nags out of the stable,
    Where they stood thirty and three.

She mounted her on her milk-white steed,
    He on the dapple grey ;
They rode till they came unto the sea side,
    Three hours before it was day.

Light off, light off thy milk-white steed,
    And deliver it unto me ;
Six pretty maids have I drownèd here,
    And thou the seventh shall be.

Pull off, pull off thy silken gown,
    And deliver it unto me,
Methinks it looks too rich and too gay
    To rot in the salt sea.

Pull off, pull off thy silken stays,
    And deliver them unto me ;
Methinks they are too fine and gay
    To rot in the salt sea.

Pull off, pull off thy Holland smock,
　　And deliver it unto me;
Methinks it looks too rich and gay,
　　To rot in the salt sea.

If I must pull off my Holland smock,
　　Pray turn thy back unto me,
For it is not fitting that such a ruffian
　　A naked woman should see.

He turned his back towards her,
　　And viewed the leaves so green,
She catched him round the middle so small,
　　And tumbled him into the stream.

He dropped high, and he dropped low,
　　Until he came to the side,
Catch hold of my hand, my pretty maiden,
　　And I will make you my bride.

Lie there, lie there, you false-hearted man,
　　Lie there instead of me;
Six pretty maids have you drownèd here,
　　And the seventh has drownèd thee.

She mounted on her milk-white steed,
　　And led the dapple gray,
She rode till she came to her own father's hall,
　　Three hours before it was day.

The parrot being in the window so high,
　　Hearing the lady, did say,
I'm afraid that some ruffian has led you astray,
　　That you have tarried so long away.

Don't prittle nor prattle, my pretty parrot,
　　Nor tell no tales of me;
Thy cage shall be made of the glittering gold,
　　Although it is made of a tree.

The king being in the chamber so high,
　　And hearing the parrot, did say,
What ails you, what ails you my pretty parrot?
　　That you prattle so long before day.

It's no laughing matter, the parrot did say,
　　But so loudly I call unto thee;
For the cats have got into the window so high,
　　And I'm afraid they will have me.

Well turned, well turned, my pretty parrot,
　　Well turned, well turned for me;
Thy cage shall be made of the glittering gold,
　　And the door of the best ivory.

VI.

Lord Lovel.

THE ballad of *Lord Lovel* is from a broadside printed in the metropolis during the present year. A version may be seen in Kinloch's *Ancient Scottish Ballads*, where it is given as taken down from the recitation of a lady in Roxburghshire. Mr. M. A. Richardson, the editor of the *Local Historian's Table Book*, says that the ballad is ancient, and the hero is traditionally believed to have been one of the family of Lovele, or Delavalle, of Northumberland: the London printers say that *their* copy is very old. The two last verses are common to many ballads. From the tune being that to which the old ditty of *Johnnie o' Cockelsmuir* is sung, it is not improbable that the story is of Northumbrian or Border origin.

LORD Lovel he stood at his castle gate,
    Combing his milk-white steed;
When up came Lady Nancy Belle,
    To wish her lover good speed, speed,
    To wish her lover good speed.

Where are you going, Lord Lovel? she said,
    Oh! where are you going? said she;
I'm going, my Lady Nancy Belle,
    Strange countries for to see, see,
    Strange countries for to see.

When will you be back, Lord Lovel? she said,
  Oh! when will you come back? said she;
In a year or two—or three, at the most,
  I'll return to my fair Nancý,-cý,
  I'll return to my fair Nancý.

But he had not been gone a year and a day,
  Strange countries for to see ;
When languishing thoughts came into his head,
  Lady Nancy Belle he would go see, see,
  Lady Nancy Belle he would go see.

So he rode, and he rode on his milk-white steed,
  Till he came to London town ;
And there he heard St. Pancras bells,
  And the people all mourning round, round,
  And the people all mourning round.

Oh! what is the matter? Lord Lovel he said,
  Oh! what is the matter? said he;
A lord's lady is dead, a woman replied,
  And some call her Lady Nancy-cy,
  And some call her Lady Nancy.

So he ordered the grave to be opened wide,
  And the shroud he turnèd down,
And there he kissed her clay-cold lips,
  Till the tears came trickling down, down,
  Till the tears came trickling down.

Lady Nancy she died, as it might be to-day,
   Lord Lovel he died as to-morrow;
Lady Nancy she died out of pure, pure grief,
   Lord Lovel he died out of sorrow, sorrow,
   Lord Lovel he died out of sorrow.

Lady Nancy was laid in St. Pancras church,
   Lord Lovel was laid in the choir;
And out of her bosom there grew a red rose,
   And out of her lover's a briar, briar,
   And out of her lover's a briar.

They grew, and they grew, to the church steeple, too,
   And then they could grow no higher;
So there they entwined in a true-lover's knot,
   For all lovers true to admire-mire,
   For all lovers true to admire.

VII.

Lord Delaware.

(TRADITIONAL.)

THIS interesting traditional ballad was first published by Mr.
Thomas Lyle in his *Ancient Ballads and Songs*, London, 1827.
" We have not as yet," says Mr. Lyle, " been able to trace out
the historical incident upon which this ballad appears to have
been founded ; yet those curious in such matters may consult, if
they list, *Proceedings and Debates in the House of Commons, for* 1621
and 1662, where they will find that some stormy debating in

these several years had been agitated in parliament regarding the
corn laws, which bear pretty close upon the leading features of
the ballad." Does not the ballad, however, belong to a much
earlier period ?   The description of the combat, the presence of
heralds, the wearing of armour, &c., induce the editor to believe
so.   For De la Ware, ought we not to read De la Mare ? and is
not Sir Thomas De la Mare the hero ? the De la Mare who in the
reign of Edward III, A.D. 1377, was speaker of the House of
Commons.   All historians are agreed in representing him as a
person using "great freedom of speach," and which, indeed, he
carried to such an extent as to endanger his personal liberty.
As bearing somewhat upon the subject of the ballad, it may be
observed that De la Mare was a great advocate of popular rights,
and particularly protested against the inhabitants of England
being subject to "purveyance," asserting that "if the royal
revenue was faithfully administered, there could be no necessity
for laying burdens on the people."   In the subsequent reign of
Richard II, De la Mare was a prominent character, and though
history is silent on the subject, it is not improbable that such a
man might, even in the royal presence, have defended the rights
of the poor, and spoken in extenuation of the agrarian insur-
rectionary movements which were then so prevalent and so
alarming.   On the hypothesis of De la Mare being the hero,
there are other incidents in the tale which cannot be reconciled
with history, as the title given to De la Mare, who certainly was
never ennobled, nor (as far as we can ascertain), ever mixed up
in any duel; nor does it appear clear who can be meant by the
"Welsh lord, the brave Duke of Devonshire," such dukedom having been only created in 1694, and no nobleman having derived
any title whatever from Devonshire previously to 1618, when
Baron Cavendish of Hardwick was created the first *Earl* of
Devonshire.   We may therefore presume that for "Devonshire"
ought to be inserted the name of some other county or place.
Strict historical accuracy is, however, hardly to be expected
in any ballad, particularly in one which like the present has
evidently been corrupted in floating down the stream of time.
There is only one quarrel recorded at the supposed period of our
tale as having taken place betwixt two noblemen, and which re-
sulted in an hostile meeting, viz., that wherein the belligerent

G

parties were the Duke of Hereford, (who might by a "ballad-monger" be deemed a *Welsh* lord), and the Duke of Norfolk. This was in the reign of Richard II. No fight, however, took place, owing to the interference of the king. Our minstrel author may have had rather confused historical ideas, and so mixed up certain passages in De la Mare's history with this squabble, and the editor is strongly induced to believe that such is the case, and will be found the real clue to the story. Vide *Hume's History of England*, chap. XVII. A.D. 1398. Lyle acknowledges that he has taken some liberties with the oral version, but does not state what they were, beyond that they consisted merely in "smoothing down ;" would that he had left it "in the *rough !*" The last verse has every appearance of being apocryphal; it looks like one of those benedictory verses with which minstrels were, and still are in the habit of concluding their songs. Lyle says the tune "is pleasing, and peculiar to the ballad."

IN the Parliament House,
    A great rout has been there,
Betwixt our good King
    And the Lord Delaware:
Says Lord Delaware
    To his Majesty full soon,
Will it please you, my liege,
    To grant me a boon ?

What's your boon, says the King,
    Now let me understand ?
It's, give me all the poor men
    We've starving in this land ;
And without delay, I'll hie me
    To Lincolnshire,
To sow hemp-seed and flax-seed,
    And hang them all there.

For with hempen cord it's better
　　To stop each poor man's breath,
Than with famine you should see
　　Your subjects starve to death.
Up starts a Dutch Lord,
　　Who to Delaware did say,
Thou deserves to be stabbed!
　　Then he turned himself away:

Thou deserves to be stabbed,
　　And the dogs have thine ears,
For insulting our King
　　In this Parliament of peers;
Up sprang a Welsh Lord,
　　The brave Duke of Devonshire,
In young Delaware's defence, I'll fight
　　This Dutch Lord, my sire.

For he is in the right,
　　And I'll make it so appear:
Him I dare to single combat,
　　For insulting Delaware.
A stage was soon erected,
　　And to combat they went,
For to kill, or to be killed,
　　It was either's full intent.

But the very first flourish,
　　When the heralds gave command,

The sword of brave Devonshire
　　Bent backward on his hand;
In suspense he paused awhile,
　　Scanned his foe before he strake,
Then against the king's armour,
　　His bent sword he brake.

Then he sprang from the stage,
　　To a soldier in the ring,
Saying, Lend your sword, that to an end
　　This tragedy we bring:
Though he's fighting me in armour,
　　While I am fighting bare,
Even more than this I'd venture
　　For young Lord Delaware.

Leaping back on the stage,
　　Sword to buckler now resounds,
Till he left the Dutch Lord
　　A bleeding in his wounds:
This seeing, cries the King
　　To his guards without delay,
Call Devonshire down,—
　　Take the dead man away!

No, says brave Devonshire,
　　I've fought him as a man,
Since he's dead, I will keep
　　The trophies I have won;

For he fought me in your armour,
 While I fought him bare,
And the same you must win back, my liege,
 If ever you them wear.

God bless the Church of England,
 May it prosper on each hand,
And also every poor man
 Now starving in this land;
And while I pray success may crown
 Our king upon his throne,
I'll wish that every poor man,
 May long enjoy his own.

VIII.

Lord Beichan.

(TRADITIONAL.)

THE history of this old Border ballad has been so fully entered
upon by the present editor in his *Scottish Traditional Versions of
Ancient Ballads*, published by the Percy Society, that it is merely
necessary to refer the reader to the notes on *Young Bondwell*, in
that work. The present version of *Lord Beichan* was originally
published in *The Local Historian's Table Book*. On referring to it
as there printed, it will be seen that in a single instance, owing
to a verse containing an absurd contradiction, when compared
with a subsequent part of the same ballad, it was necessary to make
a conjectural emendation. The true reading is now given, the
same having since been discovered in a Scottish copy. To remove
a glaring inconsistency it was only requisite to alter a single
letter!

Lord Beichan he was a noble lord,
   A noble lord of high degree ;
He shipped himself on board a ship,
   He longed strange countries for to see.

He sailèd east, and he sailèd west,
   Until he came to proud Turkey;
Where he was ta'en by a savage moor,
   Who handled him right cruellie.

For he viewed the fashions of that land;
   Their way of worship viewèd he ;
But to Mahound, or Termagant,
   Would Beichan never bend a knee.

So on each shoulder they've putten a bore,
   In each bore they've putten a tye ;
And they have made him trail the wine
   And spices on his fair bodie.

They've casten him in a donjon deep,
   Where he could neither hear nor see ;
For seven long years they've kept him there,
   Till he for hunger 's like to dee.

And in his prison a tree there grew,
   So stout and strong there grew a tree,
And unto it was Beichan chained,
   Until his life was most weary.

This Turk he had one only daughter—
   Fairer creature did eyes ne'er see ;
And every day, as she took the air,
   Near Beichan's prison passèd she.

[And bonny, meek, and mild was she,
   Tho' she was come of an ill kin ;
And oft she sighed, she knew not why,
   For him that lay the donjon in.]

O! so it fell upon a day,
   She heard young Beichan sadly sing,
[And aye and ever in her ears,
   The tones of hapless sorrow ring.]

My hounds they all go masterless ;
   My hawks they flee from tree to tree ;
My younger brother will heir my land ;
   Fair England again I'll never see.

And all night long no rest she got,
   Young Beichan's song for thinking on :
She's stown the keys from her father's head,
   And to the prison strong is gone.

And she has oped the prison doors,
   I wot she opened two or three,
Ere she could come young Beichan at,
   He was locked up so curiouslie.

But when she came young Beichan before,
   Sore wondered he that maid to see!
He took her for some fair captive,—
   Fair Ladye, I pray of what countrie?

Have you got houses? have you got lands?
   Or does Northumberland 'long to thee?
What could ye give to the fair young ladye
   That out of prison would set you free?

I have got houses, I have got lands,
   And half Northumberland 'longs to me,—
I'll give them all to the ladye fair
   That out of prison will set me free.

Near London town I have a hall,
   With other castles, two or three;
I'll give them all to the ladye fair,
   That out of prison will set me free.

Give me the troth of your right hand,
   The troth of it give unto me;
That for seven years ye'll no ladye wed,
   Unless it be along with me.

I'll give thee the troth of my right hand,
   The troth of it I'll freely gie;
That for seven years I'll stay unwed,
   For kindness thou dost shew to me.

And she has bribed the proud warder,
　　With golden store, and white monèy;
She's gotten the keys of the prison strong,
　　And she has set young Beichan free.

She's gi'en him to eat the good spice cake,
　　She's gi'en him to drink the blood red wine;
And every health she drank unto him,—
　　I wish, Lord Beichan, that you were mine.
And she's bidden him sometimes think on her,
　　That so kindly freed him out of pine.

She's broken a ring from her finger,
　　And to Beichan half of it gave she,—
Keep it to mind you of that love
　　The lady bore that set you free.

O ! she took him to her father's harbour,
　　And a ship of fame to him gave she ;
Farewell, farewell, to you, Lord Beichan,
　　Shall I e'er again you see ?

Set your foot on the good ship board,
　　And haste ye back to your own countrie;
And before seven years have an end,
　　Come back again, love, and marry me.

Now seven long years are gone and past,
　　And sore she long'd her love to see ;

For ever a voice within her breast
    Said, Beichan has broken his vow to thee;
So she's set her foot on the good ship board,
    And turned her back on her own countrie.

She sailèd east, she sailèd west,
    Till to fair England's shore came she;
Where a bonny shepherd she espied,
    Feeding his sheep upon the lea.

What news, what news, thou bonnie shepherd?
    What news hast thou to tell me?
Such news I hear, ladye, he said,
    The like was never in this countrie.

There is a weddin' in yonder hall,
    Has lasted thirty days and three;
But young Lord Beichan won't bed with his bride,
    For love of one that's ayond the sea.

She's putten her hand in her pocket,
    Gi'en him the gold and white money;
Here, tak' ye that, my bonnie boy,
    For the good news thou tell'st to me.

When she came to Lord Beichan's gate,
    She tirlèd softly at the pin;
And ready was the proud warder
    To open and let this ladye in.

When she came to Lord Beichan's castle,
   So boldly she rang the bell;
Who's there? who's there? cried the proud porter,
   Who's there? unto me come tell?

O! is this Lord Beichan's castle?
   Or is that noble lord within?
Yea, he is in the hall among them all,
   And this is the day of his weddin'.

And has he wed anither love?—
   And has he clean forgotten me?
And, sighing, said that ladye gay,
   I wish I was in my own countrie.

And she has ta'en her gay gold ring,
   That with her love she brake so free,
Gie him that, ye proud porter,
   And bid the bridegroom speak to me.

Tell him to send me a slice of bread,
   And a cup of blood red wine,
And not to forget the fair young ladye
   That did release him out of pine.

Away, and away went the proud porter,
   Away, and away, and away went he,
Until he came to Lord Beichan's presence,
   Down he fell on his bended knee.

What aileth thee, my proud porter,
　　Thou art so full of courtesie?

I've been porter at your gates,—
　　It's thirty long years now, and three,
But there stands a ladye at them now,
　　The like of her I ne'er did see.

For on every finger she has a ring,
　　And on her mid-finger she has three;
And as much gay gold above her brow
　　As would an earldom buy to me;
And as much gay cloathing round about her
　　As would buy all Northumberlea.

It's out then spak' the bride's mother,—
　　Aye, and an angry woman was she,—
Ye might have excepted the bonnie bride,
　　And two or three of our companie.

O! hold your tongue, ye silly frow,
　　Of all your folly let me be;
She's ten times fairer than the bride,
　　And all that's in your companie.

She asks one sheave of my lord's white bread,
　　And a cup of his red, red wine;
And to remember the ladye's love
　　That kindly freed him out of pine.

Lord Beichan then in a passion flew,
   And broke his sword in splinters three;
O, well a day! did Beichan say,
   That I so soon have married thee!
For it can be none but dear Saphia,
   That's cross'd the deep for love of me!

And quickly hied he down the stair,
   Of fifteen steps he made but three;
He's ta'en his bonnie love in his arms,
   And kist, and kist her tenderlie.

O! have ye taken another bride?
   And have ye quite forgotten me?
And have ye quite forgotten one
   That gave you life and libertie.

She lookèd o'er her left shoulder
   To hide the tears stood in her ee;
Now fare-thee-well, young Beichan, she says,
   I'll try to think no more on thee.

O! never, never, my Saphia,
   For surely this can never be;
Nor ever shall I wed but her
   That's done and dreed so much for me.

Then out and spak' the forenoon bride:
   My Lord, your love is changèd soon;

At morning I am made your bride,
    And another's chose, ere it be noon!

O! sorrow not, thou forenoon bride,
    Our hearts could ne'er united be;
Ye must return to your own countrie,
    A double dower I'll send with thee.

And up and spak' the young bride's mother,
    Who never was heard to speak so free,—
And so you treat my only daughter,
    Because Saphia has cross'd the sea.

I own I made a bride of your daughter,
    She's ne'er a whit the worse for me,
She came to me with her horse and saddle,
    She may go back in her coach and three.

He's ta'en Saphia by the white hand,
    And gently led her up and down;
And aye as he kist her rosy lips,
    Ye're welcome, dear one, to your own.

He's ta'en her by the milk-white hand,
    And led her to yon fountain stane;
Her name he's changèd from Saphia,
    And he's called his bonnie love Lady Jane.

Lord Beichan prepared another marriage,
    And sang with heart so full of glee,

I'll range no more in foreign countries,
   Now since my love has crossed the sea.

IX.

Lord Bateman.

THIS is a ludicrously corrupt abridgment of the preceding ballad,
being the same version which was published a few years ago by
Tilt, London, and also, according to the title-page, by Mustapha
Syried, Constantinople! under the title, of *The loving Ballad of
Lord Bateman.* It is, however, the only ancient form in which
the ballad has existed in print, and is one of the publications
mentioned in *Thackeray's Catalogue,* alluded to at page 7 of the
present work. The air printed in Tilt's edition is the one to
which the ballad is sung in the South of England, but it is totally
different to the Northern tune, which has never been published.

LORD Bateman he was a noble lord,
   A noble lord of high degree;
He shipped himself on board a ship,
   Some foreign country he would go see.

He sailèd east, and he sailèd west,
   Until he came to proud Turkèy;
Where he was taken, and put to prison,
   Until his life was almost weary.

And in this prison there grew a tree,
   It grew so stout, and grew so strong;
Where he was chainèd by the middle,
   Until his life was almost gone.

This Turk he had one only daughter,
　　The fairest creature my eyes did see;
She stole the keys of her father's prison,
　　And swore Lord Bateman she would set free.

Have you got houses? have you got lands?
　　Or does Northumberland belong to thee?
What would you give to the fair young lady
　　That out of prison would set you free?

I have got houses, I have got lands,
　　And half Northumberland belongs to me,
I'll give it all to the fair young lady
　　That out of prison would set me free.

O! then she took him to her father's hall,
　　And gave to him the best of wine;
And every health she drank unto him,
　　I wish, Lord Bateman, that you were mine.

Now in seven years I'll make a vow,
　　And seven years I'll keep it strong,
If you'll wed with no other woman,
　　I will wed with no other man.

O! then she took him to her father's harbour,
　　And gave to him a ship of fame;
Farewell, farewell to you, Lord Bateman,
　　I'm afraid I ne'er shall see you again.

Now seven long years are gone and past,
    And fourteen days, well known to thee;
She packèd up all her gay cloathing,
    And swore Lord Bateman she would go see.

But when she came to Lord Bateman's castle,
    So boldly she rang the bell ;
Who's there? who's there? cry'd the proud porter,
    Who's there ? unto me come tell.

O ! is this Lord Bateman's castle ?
    Or is his Lordship here within ?
O, yes ! O, yes ! cried the young porter,
    He's just now taken his new bride in.

O ! tell him to send me a slice of bread,
    And a bottle of the best wine ;
And not forgetting the fair young lady
    Who did release him when close confin'd.

Away, away went this young proud porter,
    Away, away, and away went he,
Until he came to Lord Bateman's chamber,
    Down on his bended knees fell he.

What news, what news, my proud young porter ?
    What news hast thou brought unto me ?
There is the fairest of all young creatures
    That ever my two eyes did see !

H

She has got rings on every finger,
　　And round one of them she has got three,
And as much gay cloathing round her middle
　　As would buy all Northumberlea.

She bids you send her a slice of bread,
　　And a bottle of the best wine;
And not forgetting the fair young lady
　　Who did release you when close confin'd.

Lord Bateman he then in a passion flew,
　　And broke his sword in splinters three;
Saying, I will give all my father's riches
　　If Sophia has crossed the sea.

Then up spoke the young bride's mother,
　　Who never was heard to speak so free,
You'll not forget my only daughter,
　　If Sophia has crossed the sea.

I own I made a bride of your daughter,
　　She's neither the better nor worse for me;
She came to me with her horse and saddle,
　　She may go back in her coach and three.

Lord Bateman prepared another marriage,
　　And sang, with heart so full of glee,
I'll range no more in foreign countries,
　　Now since Sophia has crossed the sea.

————

X.

Ṫꞕe Deaṫꞕ of Parcy Reeḃ.

(TRADITIONAL.)

THE present version of an ancient and popular Northumbrian ballad was taken down by Mr. James Telfer, of Saughtree, Liddesdale, from the chanting of Kitty Hall, an old woman who resided at Fairloans, Roxburgshire. Mr. Robert White communicated it to the *Local Historian's Table Book;* it has not appeared in any other work. "Percival, or Parcy Reed," says Mr. White, "was proprietor of Troughend, an elevated tract of land lying on the west side, and nearly in the centre of Redesdale, Northumberland. His office was to suppress and order the apprehension of thieves, and other breakers of the law; in the execution of which he incurred the displeasure of a family of brothers of the name of Hall, who were owners of Girsonsfield, a farm about two miles east from Troughend. He also drew upon himself the hostility of a band of mosstroopers, Crosier by name, some of whom he had been successful in bringing to justice." The barbarous murder of Reed by the Halls and the Crosiers, is an historical fact, and the circumstances attending it are accurately detailed in the ballad. The catastrophe is said to have occurred in the sixteenth century.

———

GOD send the land deliverance
  Frae every reaving, riding Scot:
We'll sune hae neither cow nor ewe,
  We'll sune hae neither staig nor stot.

The outlaws come frae Liddesdale,
  They herry Redesdale far and near;
The rich man's gelding it maun gang,
  They canna pass the puir man's meare.

Sure it were weel, had ilka thief
   Around his neck a halter strang;
And curses heavy may they light
   On traitors vile oursels amang.

Now Parcy Reed has Crosier ta'en,
   He has delivered him to the law;
But Crosier says he'll do waur than that,
   He'll make the tower o' Troughend fa'.

And Crosier says he will do waur—
   He will do waur if waur can be;
He'll make the bairns a' fatherless,
   And then, the land it may lie lee.

To the hunting, ho! cried Parcy Reed,
   The morning sun is on the dew;
The cauler breeze frae off the fells
   Will lead the dogs to the quarry true.

To the hunting, ho! cried Parcy Reed,
   And to the hunting he has gane;
And the three fause Ha's o' Girsonsfield
   Alang wi' him he has them ta'en.

They hunted high, they hunted low,
   By heathery hill and birken shaw;
They raised a buck on Rooken Edge,
   And blew the mort at fair Ealylawe.

They hunted high, they hunted low,
    They made the echoes ring amain;
With music sweet o' horn and hound,
    They merry made fair Redesdale glen.

They hunted high, they hunted low,
    They hunted up, they hunted down,
Until the day was past the prime,
    And it grew late in the afternoon.

They hunted high in Batinghope,
    When as the sun was sinking low,
Says Parcy then, ca' off the dogs,
    We'll bait our steeds and homeward go.

They lighted high in Batinghope,
    Atween the brown and benty ground;
They had but rested a little while,
    Till Parcy Reed was sleeping sound.

There's nane may lean on a rotten staff,
    But him that risks to get a fa';
There's nane may in a traitor trust,
    And traitors black were every Ha'.

They've stown the bridle off his steed,
    And they've put water in his lang gun;
They've fixed his sword within the sheath,
    That out again it winna come.

Awaken ye, waken ye, Parcy Reed,
　Or by your enemies be ta'en;
For yonder are the five Crosiers
　A-coming owre the Hingin'-stane.

If they be five, and we be four,
　Sae that ye stand alang wi' me,
Then every man ye will take one,
　And only leave but two to me:
We will them meet as brave men ought,
　And make them either fight or flee.

We mayna stand, we canna stand,
　We daurna stand alang wi' thee;
The Crosiers haud thee at a feud,
　And they wad kill baith thee and we.

O, turn thee, turn thee, Johnie Ha',
　O, turn thee, man, and fight wi' me;
When ye come to Troughend again,
　My gude black naig I will gie thee ;
He cost full twenty pound o' gowd,
　Atween my brother John and me.

I mayna turn, I canna turn,
　I daurna turn and fight wi' thee;
The Crosiers haud thee at a feud,
　And they wad kill baith thee and me.

O, turn thee, turn thee, Willie Ha',
　O, turn thee, man, and fight wi' me;

When ye come to Troughend again,
    A yoke o' owsen I'll gie thee.

I mayna turn, I canna turn,
    I daurna turn and fight wi' thee ;
The Crosiers haud thee at a feud,
    And they wad kill baith thee and me.

O, turn thee, turn thee, Tommy Ha'—
    O, turn now, man, and fight wi' me ;
If ever we come to Troughend again,
    My daughter Jean I'll gie to thee.

I mayna turn, I canna turn,
    I daurna turn and fight wi' thee ;
The Crosiers haud thee at a feud,
    And they wad kill baith thee and me.

O, shame upon ye, traitors a'!
    I wish your hames ye may never see ;
Ye've stown the bridle off my naig,
    And I can neither fight nor flee.

Ye've stown the bridle off my naig,
    And ye've put water i' my lang gun ;
Ye've fixed my sword within the sheath,
    That out again it winna come.

He had but time to cross himsel'—
    A prayer he hadna time to say,

Till round him came the Crosiers keen,
　　All riding graithed, and in array.

Weel met, weel met, now Parcy Reed,
　　Thou art the very man we sought;
Owre lang hae we been in your debt,
　　Now will we pay ye as we ought.

We'll pay thee at the nearest tree,
　　Where we shall hang thee like a hound.
Brave Parcy rais'd his fankit sword
　　And fell'd the foremost to the ground.

Alake, and wae for Parcy Reed—
　　Alake he was an unarmed man:
Four weapons pierced him all at once,
　　As they assailed him there and than.

They fell upon him all at once,
　　They mangled him most cruellie;
The slightest wound might caused his deid,
　　And they hae gi'en him thirty-three.
They hacket off his hands and feet,
　　And left him lying on the lee.

Now, Parcy Reed, we've paid our debt,
　　Ye canna weel dispute the tale.
The Crosiers said, and off they rade—
　　They rade the airt o' Liddesdale.

It was the hour o' gloamin' gray,
   When herds come in frae fauld and pen;
A herd he saw a huntsman lie,
   Says he, can this be Laird Troughen'?

There's some will ca' me Parcy Reed,
   And some will ca' me Laird Troughen';
It's little matter what they ca' me,
   My faes hae made me ill to ken.

There's some will ca' me Parcy Reed,
   And speak my praise in tower and town;
It's little matter what they do now,
   My life-blood rudds the heather brown.

There's some will ca' me Parcy Reed,
   And a' my virtues say and sing;
I would much rather have just now
   A draught o' water frae the spring!

The herd flang aff his clouted shoon,
   And to the nearest fountain ran;
He made his bonnet serve a cup,
   And wan the blessing o' the dying man.

Now, honest herd, ye maun do mair—
   Ye maun do mair as I ye tell;
Ye maun bear tidings to Troughend,
   And bear likewise my last farewell.

A farewell to my wedded wife,
    A farewell to my brother John,
Wha sits into the Troughend tower,
    Wi' heart as black as any stone.

A farewell to my daughter Jean,
    A farewell to my young sons five;
Had they been at their father's hand,
    I had this night been man alive.

A farewell to my followers a',
    And a' my neighbours gude at need;
Bid them think how the treacherous Ha's
    Betrayed the life o' Parcy Reed.

The laird o' Clennel bears my bow,
    The laird o' Brandon bears my brand;
Whene'er they ride i' the border side,
    They'll mind the fate o' the laird Troughend.

XI.

The Golden Globe; or the 'Squire of Tamworth.

THIS is a very popular ballad, and sung in every part of England. It is traditionally reported to be founded on an incident which occurred in the reign of Elizabeth. It has been published in the broadside form from the commencement of the eighteenth century, but is no doubt much older. It does not appear to have been inserted in any collection.

A WEALTHY young 'squire of Tamworth, we hear,
He courted a nobleman's daughter so fair ;
And for to marry her it was his intent,
All friends and relations gave their consent.

The time was appointed for the wedding day,
A young farmer chosen to give her away;
As soon as the farmer the young lady did spy,
He inflamèd her heart ; O, my heart ! she did cry.

She turned from the 'squire, but nothing she said,
Instead of being married she took to her bed;
The thought of the farmer soon run in her mind,
A way for to have him she quickly did find.

Coat, waistcoat, and breeches she then did put on,
And a hunting she went with her dog and her gun ;
She hunted all round where the farmer did dwell,
Because in her heart she did love him full well :

She oftentimes fired, but nothing she killed,
At length the young farmer came into the field;
And to discourse with him it was her intent,
With her dog and her gun to meet him she went.

I thought you had been at the wedding, she cried,
To wait on the Squire, and give him his bride.
No, sir, said the farmer, if the truth I may tell,
I'll not give her away, for I love her too well.

Suppose that the lady should grant you her love,
You know that the 'squire your rival will prove;
Why then, says the farmer, I'll take sword in hand,
By honour I'll gain her when she shall command.

It pleasèd the lady to find him so bold;
She gave him a glove that was flowered with gold,
And told him she found it when coming along,
As she was a hunting with her dog and gun.

The lady went home with a heart full of love,
And gave out a notice that she'd lost a glove;
And said, Who has found it, and brings it to me,
Whoever he is, he my husband shall be.

The farmer was pleased when he heard of the news,
With heart full of joy to the lady he goes:
Dear, honourèd lady, I've picked up your glove,
And hope you'll be pleasèd to grant me your love.

It's already granted, I will be your bride;
I love the sweet breath of a farmer, she cried.
I'll be mistress of my dairy, and milking my cow,
While my jolly brisk farmer is whistling at plough.

And when she was married she told of her fun,
How she went a hunting with her dog and gun;
And [said] now I've got him so fast in my snare,
I'll enjoy him for ever, I vow and declare.

———

XII.

𝕶ing 𝕵ames 𝕴 and the 𝕿inkler.

(TRADITIONAL.)

THE ballad of *King James I and the Tinkler* was probably written either in, or shortly after the reign of the monarch who is the hero. The incident recorded is said to be a fact, though the locality is doubtful. By some the scene is laid at Norwood, in Surrey; by others in some part of the English border. The ballad is alluded to by Percy, but is not inserted either in the *Reliques*, or in any other popular collection, being only to be found in a few broadsides and chap-books of modern date. The present version is a traditional one, taken down by the editor from the recital of Francis King. It is much superior to the common broadside edition with which it has been collated, and from which the thirteenth and fifteenth verses were obtained. The ballad is very popular on the border, and in the dales of Cumberland, Westmoreland and Craven.

———

AND now, to be brief, let's pass over the rest,
Who seldom or never were given to jest,
And come to King Jamie, the first of our throne,
A pleasanter monarch sure never was known.

As he was a hunting the swift fallow-deer,
He dropt all his nobles; and when he got clear,
In hope of some pastime away he did ride,
Till he came to an alehouse, hard by a wood-side.

And there with a tinkler he happened to meet,
And him in kind sort he so freely did greet:
Pray, thee, good fellow, what hast in thy jug,
Which under thy arm thou dost lovingly hug?

By the mass! quoth the tinkler, its nappy brown ale,
And for to drink to thee, friend, I will not fail ;
For altho' thy jacket looks gallant and fine,
I think that my two-pence as good is as thine.

By my soul! honest fellow, the truth thou hast spoke,
And straight he sat down with the tinkler to joke ;
They drank to the King, and they pledged to each other,
Who'd seen 'em had thought they were brother and
        brother.

As they were a-drinking the King pleased to say,
What news, honest fellow? come tell me, I pray ?
There's nothing of news, beyond that I hear
The King's on the border a-chasing the deer.

And truly I wish I so happy may be
Whilst he is a hunting the King I might see ;
For altho' I've travelled the land many ways
I never have yet seen a King in my days.

The King, with a hearty brisk laughter, replied,
I tell thee, good fellow, if thou canst but ride,
Thou shalt get up behind me, and I will thee bring
To the presence of Jamie, thy sovereign King.

But he'll be surrounded with nobles so gay,
And how shall we tell him from them, sir, I pray?
Thou'lt easily ken him when once thou art there;
The King will be covered, his nobles all bare.

He got up behind him and likewise his sack,
His budget of leather, and tools at his back;
They rode till they came to the merry green wood,
His nobles came round him, bareheaded they stood.

The tinkler then seeing so many appear,
He slyly did whisper the King in his ear:
Saying, They're all clothed so gloriously gay,
But which amongst them is the King, sir, I pray!

The King did with hearty good laughter, reply,
By my soul! my good fellow, it's thou or it's I!
The rest are bareheaded, uncovered all round.—
With his bag and his budget he fell to the ground,

Like one that was frightened quite out of his wits,
Then on his knees he instantly gets,
Beseeching for mercy; the King to him said,
Thou art a good fellow, so be not afraid.

Come, tell thy name? I am John of the dale,
A mender of kettles, a lover of ale.
Rise up, Sir John, I will honour thee here,—
I make thee a knight of three thousand a year!

This was a good thing for the tinkler indeed ;
Then unto the court he was sent for with speed,
Where great store of pleasure and pastime was seen,
In the royal presence of King and of Queen.

Sir John of the Dale he has land, he has fee,
At the court of the king who so happy as he ?
Yet still in his Hall hangs the tinkler's old sack,
And the budget of tools which he bore at his back.

XIII.

The Reach i' the Creel.

THIS old and very humorous ballad has long been a favorite on
both sides of the Border, but had never appeared in print till
about a year ago, when a Northumbrian gentleman printed a few
copies for private circulation, one of which he presented to the
editor.   In the present impression some trifling typographical
mistakes are corrected, and the phraseology has been rendered
uniform throughout.

A fair young May went up the street,
    Some white fish for to buy ;
And a bonny clerk's fa'n i' luve wi' her,
    And he's followed her by and by, by,
And he's followed her by and by.

O! where live ye my bonny lass,
  I pray thee tell to me;
For gin the nicht were ever sae mirk,
  I wad come and visit thee, thee;
  I wad come and visit thee.

O! my father he aye locks the door,
  My mither keeps the key ;
And gin ye were ever sic a wily wicht,
  Ye canna win in to me, me ;
  Ye canna win in to me.

But the clerk he had ae true brother,
  And a wily wicht was he ;
And he has made a lang ladder,
  Was thirty steps and three, three ;
  Was thirty steps and three.

He has made a cleek but and a creel —
  A creel but and a pin ;
And he's away to the chimley-top,
  And he's letten the bonny clerk in, in ;
  And he's letten the bonny clerk in.

The auld wife, being not asleep,
  Tho' late late was the hour;
I'll lay my life, quo' the silly auld wife,
  There's a man i' our dochter's bower, bower ;
  There's a man i' our dochter's bower.

1

The auld man he gat owre the bed,
　　To see if the thing was true;
But she's ta'en the bonny clerk in her arms,
　　And covered him owre wi' blue, blue;
　　And covered him owre wi' blue.

O! where are ye gaun now, father? she says,
　　And where are ye gaun sae late?
Ye've disturbed me in my evening prayers,
　　And O! but they were sweit, sweit;
　　And O! but they were sweit.

O! ill betide ye, silly auld wife,
　　And an ill death may ye dee;
She has the muckle buik in her arms,
　　And she's prayin' for you and me, me;
　　And she's prayin' for you and me.

The auld wife being not asleep,
　　Then something mair was said;
I'll lay my life, quo' the silly auld wife,
　　There's a man by our dochter's bed, bed;
　　There's a man by our dochter's bed.

The auld wife she gat owre the bed,
　　To see if the thing was true;
But what the wrack took the auld wife's fit?
　　For into the creel she flew, flew;
　　For into the creel she flew.

The man that was at the chimley-top,
　　Finding the creel was fu',
He wrappit the rape round his left shouther,
　　And fast to him he drew, drew;
　　And fast to him he drew.

O, help! O, help! O, hinny, noo, help!
　　O, help! O, hinny, do!
For *him* that ye aye wished me at,
　　He's carryin' me off just noo, noo;
　　He's carryin' me off just noo.

O! if the foul thief's gotten ye,
　　I wish he may keep his haud;
For a' the lee lang winter nicht,
　　Ye'll never lie in your bed, bed;
　　Ye'll never lie in your bed.

He's towed her up, he's towed her down,
　　He's towed her through an' through;
O, Gude! assist, quo' the silly auld wife,
　　For I'm just departin' noo, noo;
　　For I'm just departin' noo.

He's towed her up, he's towed her down,
　　He's gien her a richt down fa',
Till every rib i' the auld wife's side,
　　Played nick nack on the wa', wa';
　　Played nick nack on the wa'.

O! the blue, the bonny, bonny blue,
   And I wish the blue may do weel;
And every auld wife that's sae jealous o' her
        dochter,
     May she get a good keach i' the creel, creel;
     May she get a gude keach i' the creel!

XIV.

The Merry Broomfield; or The West Country Wager.

THIS old West-country ballad was one of the broadsides printed at the Aldermary press. The editor has not met with any older impression, though he has been assured that there are black-letter copies. In Scott's *Minstrelsy of the Scottish Border* is a ballad called the *Broomfield Hill*; it is a mere fragment, but is evidently taken from the present ballad, and can only be considered as one of the many modern antiques to be found in that work.

A NOBLE young 'squire that lived in the west,
   He courted a young lady gay;
And as he was merry he put forth a jest,
   A wager with her he would lay.

A wager with me, the young lady replied,
   I pray about what must it be?
If I like the humour you shan't be denied,
   I love to be merry and free.

Quoth he, I will lay you an hundred pounds,
   A hundred pounds, aye, and ten,
That a maid if you go to the merry Broomfield,
   That a maid you return not again.

I'll lay you that wager, the lady she said,
   Then the money she flung down amain,
To the merry Broomfield I'll go a pure maid,
   The same I'll return home again.

He covered her bet in the midst of the hall,
   With a hundred and ten jolly pounds;
And then to his servant he straightway did call,
   To bring forth his hawk and his hounds.

A ready obedience the servant did yield,
   And all was made ready o'er night;
Next morning he went to the merry Broomfield,
   To meet with his love and delight.

Now when he came there, having waited a while,
   Among the green broom down he lies;
The lady came to him, and could not but smile,
   For sleep then had closèd his eyes.

Upon his right hand a gold ring she secured,
   Down from her own fingers so fair;
That when he awakèd he might be assured
   His lady and love had been there.

She left him a posie of pleasant perfume,
  Then stept from the place where he lay,
Then hid herself close in the besom of broom,
  To hear what her true love did say.

He wakened and found the gold ring on his hand,
  Then sorrow of heart he was in ;
My love has been here, I do well understand,
  And this wager I now shall not win.

Oh! where was you, my goodly gosshawk,
  The which I have purchased so dear,
Why did you not waken me out of my sleep,
  When the lady, my love, was here ?

O! with my bells did I ring, master,
  And eke with my feet did I run;
And still did I cry, pray awake! master,
  She's here now, and soon will be gone.

O! where was you, my gallant greyhound,
  Whose collar is flourished with gold ;
Why hadst thou not wakened me out of my sleep,
  When thou didst my lady behold ?

Dear master, I barked with my mouth when she came,
  And likewise my collar I shook;
And told you that here was the beautiful dame,
  But no notice of me then you took.

O! where wast thou, my serving man,
   Whom I have cloathèd so fine?
If you had waked me when she was here,
   The wager then had been mine.

In the night you should have slept, master,
   And kept awake in the day;
Had you not been sleeping when hither she came,
   Then a maid she had not gone away.

Then home he returned when the wager was lost,
   With sorrow of heart, I may say;
The lady she laughed to find her love crost,—
   This was upon midsummer day.

O, 'squire! I laid in the bushes concealed,
   And heard you, when you did complain ;
And thus I have been to the merry Broomfield,
   And a maid returned back again.

Be cheerful! be cheerful! and do not repine,
   For now 'tis as clear as the sun,
The money, the money, the money is mine,
   The wager I fairly have won.

Printed in Aldermary Churchyard, Bow-lane.

XV.

Sir John Barleycorn.

THE West-country ballad of *Sir John Barleycorn* is very ancient, and being the only version which has ever been sung at English merry-makings and country feasts, can certainly set up a better claim to antiquity than any of the three ballads on the same subject to be found in Evans's *Old Ballads*; viz., *John Barleycorn*, *The Little Barleycorn*, and *Mas Mault*. Our west-country version bears the greatest resemblance to *The Little Barleycorn*, but it is very dissimilar to any of the three. Burns altered the old ditty, but on referring to his version it will be seen that his corrections and additions want the simplicity of the original, and certainly cannot be considered improvements. The common ballad does not appear to have been inserted in any of our popular collections.

THERE came three men out of the West,
    Their victory to try;
And they have taken a solemn oath,
    Poor Barleycorn should die.

They took a plough and ploughed him in,
    And harrowed clods on his head ;
And then they took a solemn oath,
    Poor Barleycorn was dead.

There he lay sleeping in the ground,
    Till rain from the sky did fall :
Then Barleycorn sprung up his head,
    And so amazed them all.

There he remained till Midsummer,
   And looked both pale and wan ;
Then Barleycorn he got a beard,
   And so became a man.

Then they sent men with scythes so sharp,
   To cut him off at knee ;
And then poor little Barleycorn,
   They served him barbarously.

Then they sent men with pitchforks strong
   To pierce him through the heart,
And like a dreadful tragedy,
   They bound him to a cart.

And then they brought him to a barn,
   A prisoner to endure ;
And so they fetched him out again,
   And laid him on the floor.

Then they set men with holly clubs,
   To beat the flesh from his bones;
But the miller he served him worse than that,
   For he ground him betwixt two stones.

O! Barleycorn is the choicest grain
   That ever was sown on land ;
It will do more than any grain,
   By the turning of your hand.

It will make a boy into a man,
　And a man into an ass;
It will change your gold into silver,
　And your silver into brass.

It will make the huntsman hunt the fox,
　That never wound his horn;
It will bring the tinker to the stocks,
　That people may him scorn.

It will make the maids stark naked dance,
　As ever they were born;
It will help them to a job by chance,—
　Well done, Barleycorn!

It will put sack into a glass,
　And claret in the can;
And it will cause a man to drink
　Till he neither can go nor stand.

Good morrow to you, modest boy,
   I thank you for your care ;
If you had been what you should have been,
   I would not have left you there.

There is a horse in my father's stable,
   He stands beyond the thorn ;
He shakes his head above the trough,
   But dares not prey [on] the corn.

There is a bird in my father's flock,
   A double comb he wears ;
He flaps his wings, and crows full loud,
   But a capon's crest he bears.

There is a flower in my father's garden,
   They call it marygold ;
The fool that will not when he may,
   He shall not when he wold.

Said the shepherd's son, as he doft his shoon,
   My feet they shall run bare,
And if ever I meet another maid,
   I rede, that maid beware.

XVII.

Saddle to Rags.

(TRADITIONAL.)

No ballad is better known in the dales of Yorkshire than *Saddle to Rags*. It has long enjoyed an extensive popularity. The present version was taken down by the editor in October 1845, from the excellent and humorous singing of his aged and respected friend, Tommy Atkinson, of Linton, in Craven, a genuine Yorkshire yeoman, who only allows this present acknowledgment on the express condition that no prefix or adjunct be made to his name, and that he be designated in print by his fellow-dalesmen's familiar appellation of Tommy Atkinson! We have not been able to discover any broadside copy of the ballad, nor can we trace it in any collection, although we have met with *The Crafty Ploughboy, or the Highwayman Outwitted*, and some others of a like description, and having nearly the same plot, but they are all very inferior to *Saddle to Rags*. The tune is *Give ear to a frolicksome ditty, or the Rant*, being the air better known as *How happy could I be with either ;* it may be found in Chappell's *National English Airs*.

————

THIS story I'm going to sing,
    I hope it will give you content,
Concerning a silly old man
      That was going to pay his rent.
        With a till da dill, till a dill, dill,
        Till a dill, dill a dill, dee,
        Sing fal de dill, dill de dill, dill,
        Fal de dill, dill de dill, dee.

As he was a-riding along,
    Along all on the highway,
A gentleman-thief overtook him,
      And thus unto him he did say:

O! well overtaken, old man,
   O! well overtaken, said he—
Thank you kindly, sir, says the old man,
   If you be for my companie.

How far are you going this way ?
   It made the old man to smile;
To tell you the truth, kind sir,
   I'm just a going twa mile.

I am but a silly old man,
   Who farms a piece of ground ;
My half year rent, kind sir,
   Just comes to forty pound.

But my landlord's not been at hame,—
   I've not seen him twelve month or more;
It makes my rent to be large,
   I've just to pay him fourscore.

You should not have told any body,
   For thieves they are ganging many :
If they were to light upon you
   They would rob you of every penny.

O! never mind, says the old man,
   Thieves I fear on no side ;
My money is safe in my bags,
   In the saddle on which I ride.

As they were a-riding along,
    And riding a-down a ghyll,
The thief pulled out a pistol,
    And bade the old man stand still.

The old man was crafty and false,
    As in this world are many ;
He flung his old saddle o'er t' hedge,
    And said, Fetch it, if thou'lt have any.

This thief got off his horse,
    With courage stout and bold,
To search this old man's bags,
    And gave him his horse to hold.

The old man put foot in stirrup,
    And he got on astride,
He set the thief's horse in a gallop,—
    You need not bid th' old man ride!

O, stay! O, stay! says the thief,
    And thou half my share shalt have ;
Nay, marry, not I, quoth the old man,
    For once I've bitten a knave !

This thief he was not content,
    He thought there *must* be bags,
So he up with his rusty sword,
    And chopped the old saddle to rags.

The old man gallop'd and rode,
    Until he was almost spent,
Till he came to his landlord's house,
    And he paid him his whole year's rent.

He opened this rogue's portmantle,
    It was glorious for to behold ;
There was five hundred pound in money,
    And other five hundred in gold.

His landlord it made him to stare,
    When he did the sight behold ;
Where did thou get the white money,
    And where get the yellow gold ?

I met a fond fool by the way,
    I swapped horses, and gave him no boot;
But never mind, says the old man,
    I got a fond fool by the foot.

But now you're grown cramped and old,
    Nor fit for to travel about :
O, never mind, says the old man,
    I can give these old bones a root!

As he was a-riding hame,
    And a-down a narrow lane,
He spied his mare tied to a tree,
    And said, Tib, thou'lt now gae hame.

K

And when that he got hame,
　　And told his old wife what he'd done;
She rose and she donned her clothes,
　　And about the house did run.

She sung, and she danced, and sung,
　　And she sung with a merry devotion,
If ever our daughter gets wed,
　　It will help to enlarge her portion !

———

XVIII.

Ｔ𝔥𝔢 𝔅𝔢𝔞𝔲𝔱𝔦𝔣𝔲𝔩 𝔏𝔞𝔡𝔶 𝔬𝔣 𝔎𝔢𝔫𝔱 :

Or, The Seaman of Dover.

THE editor has met with two copies of this genuineEnglish ballad ; the older one is without printer's name, but from the appearance of the type and the paper, it must have been published about the middle of the last century.   It is certainly not one of the original impressions, for the other copy, though of recent date, has evidently been taken from some much older and better edition than any which has come to our hands.   In the modern broadside the ballad is in four parts, whereas, in our older .one, there is no such division, but a word at the commencement of each part is printed in capital letters.

———

PART I.

A SEAMAN of Dover, whose excellent parts,
For wisdom and learning, had conquered the hearts
Of many young damsels, of beauty so bright,
Of him this new ditty in brief I shall write ;

And shew of his turnings, and windings of fate,
His passions and sorrows, so many and great:
And how he was blessèd with true love at last,
When all the rough storms of his troubles were past.

Now, to be brief, I shall tell you the truth:
A beautiful lady, whose name it was Ruth,
A 'squire's young daughter, near Sandwich, in Kent,
Proves all his heart's treasure, his joy and content.

Unknown to their parents in private they meet,
Where many love lessons they'd often repeat,
With kisses, and many embraces likewise,
She granted him love, and thus gainèd the prize.

She said, I consent to be thy sweet bride,
Whatever becomes of my fortune, she cried.
The frowns of my father I never will fear,
But freely will go through the world with my dear.

A jewel he gave her, in token of love,
And vowed, by the sacred powers above,
To wed the next morning; but they were betrayed,
And all by the means of a treacherous maid.

She told her parents that they were agreed:
With that they fell into a passion with speed,
And said, ere a seaman their daughter should have,
They rather would follow her corpse to the grave.

The lady was straight to her chamber confined,
Here long she continued in sorrow of mind,

And so did her love, for the loss of his dear,—
No sorrow was ever so sharp and severe.

When long he had mourned for his love and delight,
Close under the window he came in the night,
And sung forth this ditty:—My dearest, farewell!
Behold, in this nation no longer I dwell.

I am going from thence to the kingdom of Spain;
Because I am willing that you should obtain
Your freedom once more; for my heart it will break
If longer thou liest confined for my sake.

The words which he uttered, they caused her to weep,
Yet, nevertheless, she was forcèd to keep
Deep silence that minute, that minute for fear
Her honourèd father and mother should hear.

PART II.

Soon after, bold Henry he entered on board,
The heavens a prosperous gale did afford,
And brought him with speed to the kingdom of Spain,
There he with a merchant some time did remain;

Who, finding that he was both faithful and just,
Preferred him to places of honour and trust;
He made him as great as his heart could request,
Yet, wanting his Ruth, he with grief was opprest.

So great was his grief it could not be concealed,
Both honour and riches no pleasure could yield;

In private he often would weep and lament,
For Ruth, the fair, beautiful lady of Kent.

Now, while he lamented the loss of his dear,
A lady of Spain did before him appear,
Bedecked with rich jewels both costly and gay,
Who earnestly sought for his favour that day.

Said she, Gentle swain, I am wounded with love,
And you are the person I honour above
The greatest of nobles that ever was born ;—
Then pity my tears, and my sorrowful mourn!

I pity thy sorrowful tears, he replied,
And wish I were worthy to make thee my bride ;
But, lady, thy grandeur is greater than mine,
Therefore, I am fearful my heart to resign.

O! never be doubtful of what will ensue,
No manner of danger will happen to you ;
At my own disposal I am, I declare,
Receive me with love, or destroy me with care.

Dear madam, don't fix your affection on me,
You are fit for some lord of a noble degree,
That is able to keep up your honour and fame;
I am but a poor sailor, from England who came.

A man of mean fortune, whose substance is small,
I have not wherewith to maintain you withall,
Sweet lady, according to honour and state;
Now this is the truth, which I freely relate.

The lady she lovingly squeezèd his hand,
And said with a smile, Ever blessed be the land

That bred such a noble, brave seaman as thee;
I value no honours, thou'rt welcome to me;

My parents are dead, I have jewels untold,
Besides in possession a million of gold ;
And thou shalt be lord of whatever I have,
Grant me but thy love, which I earnestly crave.

Then, turning aside, to himself he replied,
I am courted with riches and beauty beside ;
This love I may have, but my Ruth is denied.
Wherefore he consented to make her his bride.

The lady she cloathèd him costly and great;
His noble deportment, both proper and straight,
So charmèd the innocent eye of his dove,
And added a second new flame to her love.

Then married they were without longer delay ;
Now here we will leave them both glorious and gay,
To speak of fair Ruth, who in sorrow was left
At home with her parents, of comfort bereft.

PART III.

WHEN under the window with an aching heart,
He told his fair Ruth he so soon must depart,
Her parents they heard, and well pleasèd they were,
But Ruth was afflicted with sorrow and care.

Now, after her lover had quitted the shore,
They kept her confined a full twelvemonth or more,

And then they were pleasèd to set her at large,
With laying upon her a wonderful charge.

To fly from a seaman as she would from death,
She promised she would, with a faltering breath;
Yet, nevertheless, the truth you shall hear,
She found out a way for to follow her dear:

Then, taking her gold and her silver alsò,
In seaman's apparel away she did go,
And found out a master, with whom she agreed,
To carry her over the ocean with speed.

Now, when she arrived at the kingdom of Spain,
From city to city she travelled amain,
Enquiring about everywhere for her love,
Who now had been gone seven years and above.

In Cadiz, as she walked along in the street,
Her love and his lady she happened to meet,
But in such a garb as she never had seen,—
She looked like an angel, or beautiful queen.

With sorrowful tears she turned her aside:
My jewel is gone, I shall ne'er be his bride;
But, nevertheless, though my hopes are in vain,
I'll never return to old England again.

But here, in this place, I will now be confined;
It will be a comfort and joy to my mind,
To see him sometimes, though he thinks not of me,
Since he has a lady of noble degree.

Now, while in the city fair Ruth did reside,
Of a sudden this beautiful lady she died,

And, though he was in the possession of all,
Yet tears from his eyes in abundance did fall.

As he was expressing his piteous moan,
Fair Ruth came unto him, and made herself known;
He started to see her, but seemèd not coy,
Said he, Now my sorrows are mingled with joy!

The time of the mourning he kept it in Spain,
And then he came back to old England again,
With thousands, and thousands, which he did possess;
Then glorious and gay was sweet Ruth in her dress.

———

PART IV.

When over the seas to fair Sandwich he came,
With Ruth, and a number of persons of fame,
Then all did appear most splendid and gay,
As if it had been a great festival day.

Now, when that they took up their lodgings, behold!
He stript off his coat of embroiderèd gold,
And presently borrows a mariner's suit,
That he with her parents might have some dispute,

Before they were sensible he was so great.
And when he came in and knocked at the gate,
He soon saw her father, and mother likewise,
Expressing their sorrow with tears in their eyes:

To them, with obeisance, he modestly said,
Pray where is my jewel, that innocent maid,

Whose sweet lovely beauty doth thousands excell ?—
I fear, by your weeping, that all is not well!

No, no! she is gone, she is utterly lost;
We have not heard of her a twelvemonth at most!
Which makes us distracted with sorrow and care,
And drowns us in tears at the point of despair.

I'm grievèd to hear these sad tidings, he cried.
Alas! honest young man, her father replied,
I heartily wish she'd been wedded to you,
For then we this sorrow had never gone through.

Sweet Henry he made them this answer again;
I am newly come home from the kingdom of Spain,
From whence I have brought me a beautiful bride,
And am to be married to-morrow, he cried;

And if you will go to my wedding, said he,
Both you and your lady right welcome shall be.
They promised they would, and accordingly came,
Not thinking to meet with such persons of fame.

All decked with their jewels of rubies and pearls,
As equal companions of lords and of earls,
Fair Ruth, with her love, was as gay as the rest,
So they in their marriage were happily blest.

Now, as they returned from the church to an inn,
The father and mother of Ruth did begin
Their daughter to know, by a mole they behold,
Although she was cloathed in a garment of gold.

With transports of joy they flew to the bride,
O! where hast thou been, sweetest daughter? they cried,

Thy tedious absence has grievèd us sore,
As fearing, alas! we should see thee no more.

Dear parents, said she, many hazards I run,
To fetch home my love, and your dutiful son ;
Receive him with joy, for 'tis very well known,
He seeks not your wealth, he's enough of his own.

Her father replied, and he merrily smiled,
He 's brought home enough, as he 's brought home my
        child ;
A thousand times welcome you are, I declare,
Whose presence disperses both sorrow and care.

Full seven long days in feasting they spent ;
The bells in the steeple they merrily went,
And many fair pounds were bestowed on the poor,—
The like of this wedding was never before !

XIX.

The Berkshire Lady's Garland.

IN FOUR PARTS.

To the tune of *The Royal Forester.*

WHEN we first met with this very pleasing English ballad, we
deemed the story to be wholly fictitious, but " strange" as the
" relation" may appear, the incidents narrated are " true" or at least
founded on fact. The scene of the ballad is Whitley Park, near
Reading, in Berkshire, and not, as some suppose, Calcot House,
which was only built in 1759. Whitley is mentioned by Leland as
" the Abbot's Park, being at the entrance of Redding town." At
the Dissolution the estate passed to the crown, and the mansion

seems, from time to time, to have been used as a royal " palace"
till the reign of Elizabeth, by whom it was granted, along with
the estate, to Sir Francis Knollys; it was afterwards, by purchase, the property of the Kendricks, an ancient race descended
from the Saxon kings. William Kendrick, of Whitley, arm.
was created a baronet in 1679, and died in 1685, leaving issue
one son, Sir William Kendrick, of Whitley, Bart., who married
Miss Mary House, of Reading, and died in 1699, without issue
male, leaving an only daughter. It was this rich heiress, who
possessed "store of wealth and beauty bright," that is the
heroine of the ballad. She married Benjamin Child, Esq., a
young and handsome, but very poor attorney of Reading, and
the marriage is traditionally reported to have been brought about
exactly as related in the ballad. The editor has not been able
to ascertain the date of the marriage, which was celebrated in
St. Mary's Church, Reading, the bride wearing a thick veil, but
the ceremony must have taken place some time about 1705. In
1714, Mr. Child was high sheriff of Berkshire. As he was a
humble and obscure personage previously to his espousing the
heiress of Whitley, and, in fact, owed all his wealth and influence to such marriage, it cannot be supposed that *immediately*
after his union he would be elevated to so important and dig-
nified a post as the high-shrievalty of the very aristocratical
county of Berks. We may, therefore, consider nine or ten
years to have e'apsed betwixt his marriage and his holding
the office of high sheriff, which he filled when he was about
thirty-two years of age. The author of the ballad is unknown:
supposing him to have composed it shortly after the events
which he records, we cannot be far wrong in fixing its date
about 1706. The earliest broadside we have met with contains a
rudely executed, but by no means bad likeness of Queen Anne,
the reigning monarch at that period.

PART I.

SHEWING CUPID'S CONQUEST OVER A COY LADY OF FIVE
THOUSAND A YEAR.

BACHELORS of every station,
Mark this strange and true relation,
Which in brief to you I bring,—
Never was a stranger thing!

You shall find it worth the hearing;
Loyal love is most endearing,
When it takes the deepest root,
Yielding charms and gold to boot.

Some will wed for love of treasure;
But the sweetest joy and pleasure
Is in faithful love, you'll find,
Gracèd with a noble mind.

Such a noble disposition
Had this lady, with submission,
Of whom I this sonnet write,
Store of wealth, and beauty bright.

She had left, by a good grannum,
Full five thousand pounds per annum,
Which she held without control ;
Thus she did in riches roll.

Though she had vast store of riches,
Which some persons much bewitches,
Yet she bore a virtuous mind,
Not the least to pride inclined.

Many noble persons courted
This young lady, 'tis reported ;
But their labour proved in vain,
They could not her favour gain.

Though she made a strong resistance,
Yet by Cupid's true assistance,

She was conquered after all;
How it was declare I shall.

Being at a noble wedding,
Near the famous town of Redding,
A young gentleman she saw,
Who belongèd to the law.

As she viewed his sweet behaviour,
Every courteous carriage gave her
New addition to her grief;
Forced she was to seek relief.

Privately she then enquirèd
About him, so much admirèd;
Both his name, and where he dwelt,—
Such was the hot flame she felt.

Then, at night, this youthful lady
Called her coach, which being ready,
Homewards straight she did return,
But her heart with flames did burn.

———

PART II.

SHEWING THE LADY'S LETTER OF A CHALLENGE TO FIGHT
HIM UPON HIS REFUSING TO WED HER IN A MASK,
WITHOUT KNOWING WHO SHE WAS.

Night and morning, for a season,
In her closet would she reason
With herself, and often said,
Why has love my heart betrayed?

I, that have so many slighted,
Am at length so well requited;
For my griefs are not a few!
Now I find what love can do.

He that has my heart in keeping,
Though I for his sake be weeping,
Little knows what grief I feel;
But I'll try it out with steel.

For I will a challenge send him,
And appoint where I'll attend him,
In a grove, without delay,
By the dawning of the day.

He shall not the least discover
That I am a virgin lover,
By the challenge which I send;
But for justice I contend.

He has causèd sad distraction,
And I come for satisfaction,
Which if he denies to give,
One of us shall cease to live.

Having thus her mind revealèd,
She her letter closed and sealèd;
Which, when it came to his hand,
The young man was at a stand.

In her letter she conjured him
For to meet, and well assured him,
Recompense he must afford,
Or dispute it with the sword.

Having read this strange relation,
He was in a consternation;
But advising with his friend,
He persuades him to attend.

Be of courage, and make ready,
Faint heart never won fair lady;
In regard it must be so,
I along with you must go.

PART III.

SHEWING HOW THEY MET BY APPOINTMENT IN A GROVE, WHERE SHE OBLIGED HIM TO FIGHT OR WED HER.

EARLY on a summer's morning,
When bright Phœbus was adorning
Every bower with his beams,
The fair lady came, it seems.

At the bottom of a mountain,
Near a pleasant crystal fountain,
There she left her gilded coach,
While the grove she did approach.

Covered with her mask, and walking,
There she met her lover talking
With a friend that he had brought;
So she asked him whom he sought.

I am challenged by a gallant,
Who resolves to try my talent;
Who he is I cannot say,
But I hope to shew him play.

It is I that did invite you,
You shall wed me, or I'll fight you,
Underneath those spreading trees;
Therefore, choose you which you please.

You shall find I do not vapour,
I have brought my trusty rapier;
Therefore, take your choice, said she,
Either fight or marry me.

Said he, Madam, pray what mean you?
In my life I've never seen you;
Pay unmask, your visage show,
Then I'll tell you aye or no.

I will not my face uncover
Till the marriage ties are over;
Therefore, choose you which you will,
Wed me, sir, or try your skill.

Step within that pleasant bower,
With your friend one single hour;
Strive your thoughts to reconcile,
And I'll wander here the while.

While this beauteous lady waited,
The young bachelors debated
What was best for to be done:
Quoth his friend, The hazard run.

If my judgment can be trusted,
Wed her first, you can't be worsted;
If she's rich, you'll rise to fame,
If she's poor, why! you're the same.

He consented to be married;
All three in a coach were carried
To a church without delay,
Where he weds the lady gay.

Tho' sweet pretty Cupids hovered
Round her eyes, her face was covered
With a mask,—he took her thus,
Just for better or for worse.

With a courteous kind behaviour,
She presents his friend a favour,
And withal dismissed him straight,
That he might no longer wait.

———

PART IV.

SHEWING HOW THEY RODE TOGETHER IN HER GILDED COACH TO HER NOBLE SEAT, OR CASTLE, ETC.

As the gilded coach stood ready,
The young lawyer and his lady
Rode together, till they came
To her house of state and fame;

Which appearèd like a castle,
Where you might behold a parcel
Of young cedars, tall and straight,
Just before her palace gate.

Hand in hand they walked together,
To a hall, or parlour, rather,
Which was beautiful and fair,—
All alone she left him there.

L

Two long hours there he waited
Her return,—at length he fretted,
And began to grieve at last,
For he had not broke his fast.

Still he sat like one amazèd,
Round a spacious room he gazèd,
Which was richly beautified ;
But, alas! he lost his bride.

There was peeping, laughing, sneering,
All within the lawyer's hearing ;
But his bride he could not see ;
Would I were at home! thought he.

While his heart was melancholy,
Said the steward, brisk and jolly,
Tell me, friend, how came you here ?
You've some bad design, I fear.

He replied, dear loving master,
You shall meet with no disaster
Through my means, in any case,—
Madam brought me to this place.

Then the steward did retire,
Saying, that he would enquire
Whether it was true or no:
Ne'er was lover hampered so.

Now the lady who had filled him
With those fears, full well beheld him

From a window, as she drest,
Pleasèd at the merry jest.

When she had herself attirèd
In rich robes, to be admirèd,
She appearèd in his sight,
Like a moving angel bright.

Sir! my servants have related,
How some hours you have waited
In my parlour,—tell me who
In my house you ever knew?

Madam! if I have offended,
It is more than I intended;
A young lady brought me here:—
That is true, said she, my dear.

I can be no longer cruel
To my joy, and only jewel;
Thou art mine, and I am thine,
Hand and heart I do resign!

Once I was a wounded lover,
Now these fears are fairly over;
By receiving what I gave,
Thou art lord of what I have.

Beauty, honour, love, and treasure,
A rich golden stream of pleasure,
With his lady he enjoys;
Thanks to Cupid's kind decoys.

Now he's cloathed in rich attire,
Not inferior to a 'squire;
Beauty, honour, riches' store,
What can man desire more?

XX.

The Nobleman's Generous Kindness.

Giving an account of a nobleman, who taking notice of a poor
man's industrious care and pains for the maintaining of his
charge of seven small children, met him upon a day, and dis-
coursing with him, invited him, and his wife and his children,
home to his house, and bestowed upon them a farm of thirty
acres of land, to be continued to him and his heirs for ever.

To the tune of *The Two English Travellers.*

THIS pleasing ballad is entitled in the modern copies, *The Nobleman and Thrasher; or the Generous Gift.* It is very popular at
the present day. There is a copy preserved in the Roxburgh
Collection, with which our imprint has been collated. The tune
to which the editor has always heard the ballad sung is *Derry
Down.*

A NOBLEMAN lived in a village of late,
Hard by a poor thrasher, whose charge it was great;
For he had seven children, and most of them small,
And nought but his labour to support them withall.

He never was given to idle and lurk,
For this nobleman saw him go daily to work,
With his flail and his bag, and his bottle of beer,
As cheerful as those that have hundreds a year.

Thus careful, and constant, each morning he went,
Unto his daily labour with joy and content;
So jocular and jolly he'd whistle and sing,
As blithe and as brisk as the birds in the spring.

One morning, this nobleman taking a walk,
He met this poor man, and he freely did talk;
He asked him, [at first], many questions at large,
And then began talking concerning his charge.

Thou hast many children, I very well know,
Thy labour is hard, and thy wages are low,
And yet thou art cheerful; I pray tell me true,
How can you maintain them as well as you do?

I carefully carry home what I do earn,
My daily expenses by this I do learn;
And find it is possible, though we be poor,
To still keep the ravenous wolf from the door.

I reap and I mow, and I harrow and sow,
Sometimes a hedging and ditching I go;
No work comes amiss, for I thrash, and I plough,
Thus my bread I do earn by the sweat of my brow.

My wife she is willing to pull in a yoke,
We live like two lambs, nor each other provoke;
We both of us strive, like the labouring ant,
And do our endeavours to keep us from want.

And when I come home from my labour at night,
To my wife and my children, in whom I delight;

To see them come round me with prattling noise,—
Now these are the riches a poor man enjoys.

Though I am as weary as weary may be,
The youngest I commonly dance on my knee;
I find that content is a moderate feast,
I never repine at my lot in the least.

Now, the nobleman hearing what he did say,
Was pleased, and invited him home the next day;
His wife and his children he charged him to bring;
In token of favour he gave him a ring.

He thankèd his honour, and taking his leave,
He went to his wife, who would hardly believe
But this same story himself he might raise;
Yet seeing the ring she was in amaze.

Betimes in the morning the good wife she arose,
And made them all fine, in the best of their clothes;
The good man with his good wife, and children small,
They all went to dine at the nobleman's hall.

But when they came there, as truth does report,
All things were prepared in a plentiful sort;
And they at the nobleman's table did dine,
With all kinds of dainties, and plenty of wine.

The feast being over, he soon let them know,
That he then intended on them to bestow
A farm-house, with thirty good acres of land,
And gave them the writings then, with his own hand.

Because thou art careful, and good to thy wife,
I'll make thy days happy the rest of thy life;
It shall be for ever, for thee and thy heirs,
Because I beheld thy industrious cares.

No tongue then is able in full to express
The depth of their joy, and true thankfulness;
With many a curtsey, and bow to the ground,—
Such noblemen there are but few to be found.

Newcastle: printed and sold by Robert Marchbank.

XXI.

The Drunkard's Legacy.

IN THREE PARTS.

First, giving an account of a gentleman's having a wild son, and who, foreseeing he would come to poverty, had a cottage built with one door to it, always kept fast; and how, on his dying bed, he charged him not to open it till he was poor and slighted, which the young man promised he would perform. Secondly, of the young man's pawning his estate to a vintner, who, when poor, kicked him out of doors; when thinking it time to see his legacy, he broke open the cottage door, where instead of money he found a gibbet and halter, which he put round his neck, and jumping off the stool, the gibbet broke, and a thousand pounds came down upon his head, which lay hid in the ceiling. Thirdly, of his redeeming his estate, and fooling the vintner out of two hundred pounds; who, for being jeered by his neighbours, cut his own throat. And lastly, of the young man's reformation. Very proper to be read by all who are given to drunkenness.

PERCY, in the introductory remarks to the ballad of *The Heir of Linne*, says, " the original of this ballad, [*The Heir of Linne*] is found in the editor's folio MS.; the breaches and defects of which rendered the insertion of supplemental stanzas necessary. These it is hoped the reader will pardon, as, indeed, the completion of the story was suggested by a modern ballad on a similar subject." The ballad thus alluded to by Percy is *The Drunkard's Legacy*, which, it may be remarked, although styled by him a *modern* ballad, is only so comparatively speaking; for it must have been written long anterior to Percy's time, and, by his own confession, must be older than the latter portion of the *Heir of Linne*. Our copy is taken from an old chap-book, without date or printer's name, and which is decorated with three rudely executed wood-cuts.

———

YOUNG people all, I pray draw near,
And listen to my ditty here;
Which subject shews that drunkenness
Brings many mortals to distress.

As, for example, now I can
Tell you of one, a gentleman,
Who had a very good estate,
His earthly travails they were great.

We understand he had one son
Who a lewd wicked race did run;
He daily spent his father's store,
When moneyless, he came for more.

The father oftentimes with tears,
Would this alarm sound in his ears;
Son! thou dost all my comfort blast,
And thou wilt come to want at last.

The son these words did little mind,
To cards and dice he was inclined;
Feeding his drunken appetite
In taverns, which was his delight.

The father, ere it was too late,
He had a project in his pate,
Before his aged days were run,
To make provision for his son.

Near to his house, we understand,
He had a waste plat of land,
Which did but little profit yield,
On which he did a cottage build.

The *Wise-Man's Project* was its name,
There were few windows in the same;
Only one door, substantial thing,
Shut by a lock, went by a spring.

Soon after he had played this trick,
It was his lot for to fall sick ;
As on his bed he did lament,
Then for his drunken son he sent.

He shortly came to his bed-side;
Seeing his son, he thus replied:
I have sent for you to make my will,
Which you must faithfully fulfil.

In such a cottage is one door,
Ne'er open it, do thou be sure,

Until thou art so poor, that all
Do then despise you, great and small.

For, to my grief, I do perceive,
When I am dead, this life you live
Will soon melt all thou hast away;
Do not forget these words, I pray.

When thou hast made thy friends thy foes,
Pawned all thy lands, and sold thy cloathes;
Break ope the door, and there depend
To find something thy griefs to end.

Thus being spoke, the son did say,
Your dying words I will obey.
Soon after this his father dear
Did die, and buried was, we hear.

PART II.

Now, pray observe the second part,
And you shall hear his sottish heart;
He did the tavern so frequent,
Till he three hundred pounds had spent.

This being done, we understand
He pawned the deeds of all his land
Unto a tavern-keeper, who
When poor, did him no favour shew.

For, to fulfil his father's will,
He did command this cottage still:

At length great sorrow was his share,
Quite moneyless, with garments bare.

Being not able for to work,
He in the tavern there did lurk;
From box to box, among rich men,
Who oftentimes reviled him then.

To see him sneak so up and down,
The vintner on him he did frown ;
And one night kicked him out of door,
Charging him to come there no more.

He in a stall did lie all night,
In this most sad and wretched plight ;
Then thought it was high time to see
His father's promised legacy.

Next morning, then, opprest with woe,
This young man got an iron crow ;
And, as in tears he did lament,
Unto this little cottage went.

When he the door had open got,
This poor, distressèd, drunken sot,
Who did for store of money hope,
He saw a gibbet and a rope.

Under this rope was placed a stool,
Which made him look just like a fool ;
Crying, Alas! what shall I do ?
Destruction now appears in view!

As my father foresaw this thing,
What sottishness to me would bring ;
As moneyless, and free of grace,
His legacy I will embrace.

So then, oppressed with discontent,
Upon the stool he sighing went ;
And then, his precious life to check,
Did place the rope about his neck.

Crying, Thou, God, who sitt'st on high,
And on my sorrow casts an eye ;
Thou knowest that I've not done well,—
Preserve my precious soul from hell.

'Tis true the slighting of thy grace,
Has brought me to this wretched case ;
And as through folly I'm undone,
I'll now eclipse my morning sun.

When he with sighs these words had spoke,
Jumped off, and down the gibbet broke ;
In falling, as it plain appears,
Dropped down about this young man's ears,

In shining gold, a thousand pound !
Which made the blood his ears surround:
Though in amaze, he cried, I'm sure
This golden salve will cure the sore !

Blest be my father, then, he cried,
Who did this part for me so hide ;

And while I do alive remain,
I never will get drunk again.

———

PART III.

Now, by the third part you will hear,
This young man, as it doth appear,
With care he then secured his chink,
And to this vintner's went to drink.

When the proud vintner did him see,
He frowned on him immediately,
And said, Begone! or else with speed,
I'll kick thee out of doors, indeed.

Smiling, the young man he did say,
Thou cruel knave! tell me, I pray,
As I have here consumed my store,
How durst thee kick me out of door?

To me thou hast been too severe;
The deeds of eight-score pounds a-year,
I pawned them for three hundred pounds,
That I spent here;—what makes such frowns?

The vintner said unto him, Sirrah!
Bring me one hundred pounds to-morrow
By nine o'clock,—take them again ;
So get you out of doors till then.

He answered, If this chink I bring,
I fear thou wilt do no such thing.

He said, I'll give under my hand,
A note, that I to this will stand.

Having the note, away he goes,
And straightway went to one of those
That made him drink when moneyless,
And did the truth to him confess.

They both went to this heap of gold,
And in a bag he fairly told
A thousand pounds, in yellow-boys,
And to the tavern went their ways.

This bag they on the table set,
Making the vintner for to fret;
He said, Young man! this will not do,
For I was but in jest with you.

So then bespoke the young man's friend:
Vintner! thou mayest sure depend,
In law this note it will you cast,
And he must have his land at last.

This made the vintner to comply,—
He fetched the deeds immediately;
He had one hundred pounds, and then
The young man got his deeds again.

At length the vintner 'gan to think
How he was fooled out of his chink;
Said, When 'tis found how I came off,
My neighbours will me game and scoff.

So to prevent their noise and clatter
The vintner he, to mend the matter,
In two days after, it doth appear,
He cut his throat from ear to ear.

Thus he untimely left the world,
That to this young man proved a churl.
Now he who followed drunkenness,
Lives sober, and doth lands possess.

Instead of wasting of his store,
As formerly, resolves no more
To act the same, but does indeed
Relieve all those that are in need.

Let all young men now, for my sake,
Take care how they such havock make;
For drunkenness, you plain may see,
Had like his ruin for to be.

ANCIENT POEMS, BALLADS, &c.

SONGS.

I.

Arthur O'Bradley's Wedding.

IN the ballad called *Robin Hood, his Birth, Breeding, Valour, and Marriage*, occurs the following line:—

"And some singing Arthur-a-Bradley."

Antiquaries are by no means agreed as to what is the song of *Arthur-a-Bradley*, there alluded to, for it so happens that there are no less than three different songs about this same Arthur-a-Bradley. Ritson gives one of them in his *Robin Hood*, commencing thus :—

"See you not Pierce the piper."

He took it from a black-letter copy in a private collection, compared with, and very much corrected by, a copy, contained in *An Antidote against Melancholy, made up in pills compounded of witty Ballads, jovial Songs, and merry Catches*, 1661. Ritson quotes another, and apparently much more modern song on the same subject, and to the same tune, beginning,—

"All in the merry month of May,"

it is a miserable composition, as may be seen by referring to a copy preserved in the third volume of the Roxburgh Ballads. There is another song, the one given by us, which appears to be as ancient as any of those of which Arthur O'Bradley is the hero, and from its subject being a wedding, as well as from its being the only Arthur O'Bradley song that we have been enabled to trace in broadside and chap-books of the last century, we are induced to believe that it may be *the* song mentioned in the old ballad, which is supposed to have been written in the reign of Charles I. An obscure music publisher, who about thirty years ago resided in the Metropolis, brought out an edition of *Arthur O'Bradley's Wedding*, with the prefix "Written by Mr. Taylor." This Mr. Taylor was, however, only a low comedian of the day, and the ascribed authorship was a mere trick on the publisher's part to increase the sale of the song. We are not able to give any account of the hero, but from his being alluded to by so many of our old writers, he was, perhaps, not altogether a fictitious personage. Ben Jonson alludes to him in one of his plays, and he is also mentioned in Decker's *Honest Whore*. Of one of the tunes mentioned in the song, viz., *Hence, Melancholy!* we can give no account; the other, *Mad Moll*, may be found in Playford's *Dancing-Master*, 1698: it is the same tune as the one known by the names of *Yellow Stockings* and *The Virgin Queen;* the latter title seeming to connect it with Queen Elizabeth, as the name of Mad Moll does with the history of Mary, who was subject to mental aberration. The words of *Mad Moll* are not known to exist, but probably consisted of some fulsome panegyric on the virgin queen, at the expense of her unpopular sister. From the mention of *Hence, Melancholy*, and *Mad Moll*, it is presumed that they were both popular favourites when *Arthur O'Bradley's Wedding* was written.

———

COME, neighbours, and listen awhile,
If ever you wishèd to smile,
Or hear a true story of old,
Attend to what I now unfold!
'Tis of a lad whose fame did resound
Through every village and town around,
For fun, for frolic, and for whim,
None ever was to equal him,
And his name was Arthur O'Bradley!
 O! rare Arthur O'Bradley! wonderful Arthur
  O'Bradley!
 Sweet Arthur O'Bradley, O!

M

Now, Arthur being stout and bold,
And near upon thirty years old,
He needs a wooing would go,
To get him a helpmate, you know.
So, gaining young Dolly's consent,
Next to be married they went;
And to make himself noble appear,
He mounted the old padded mare ;
He chose her because she was blood,
And the prime of his old daddy's stud.
She was wind-galled, spavined, and blind,
And had near lost a leg behind;
She was cropped, and docked, and fired,
And seldom, if ever, was tired:
She had such an abundance of bone;
So he called her his high-bred roan,
A credit to Arthur O'Bradley!
   O! rare Arthur O'Bradley! wonderful Arthur
      O'Bradley!
   Sweet Arthur O'Bradley, O!

Then he packed up his drudgery hose,
And put on his holiday cloaths;
His coat was of scarlet so fine,
Full trimmed with buttons behind ;
Two sleeves it had it is true,
One yellow, the other was blue,
And the cuffs and the capes were of green,
And the longest that ever were seen:
His hat, though greasy and tore,

Cocked up with a feather before,
And under his chin it was tied,
With a strip from an old cow's hide:
His breeches three times had been turned,
And two holes through the left side were burned:
Two boots he had, but not kin,
One leather, the other was tin;
And for stirrups he had two patten rings,
Tied fast to the girth with two strings:
Yet he wanted a good saddle cloth,
Which long had been eat by the moth.
'Twas a sad misfortune, you'll say,
But still he looked gallant and gay,
And his name it was Arthur O'Bradley!
   O! rare Arthur O'Bradley! wonderful Arthur
      O'Bradley!
   Sweet Arthur O'Bradley, O!

Thus accoutred, away he did ride,
While Dolly she walked by his side;
Till coming up to the church door,
In the midst of five thousand or more,
Then from the old mare he did alight,
Which put the clerk in a fright;
And the parson so fumbled and shook,
That presently down dropped his book,
Which Arthur soon picked up again,
And swore if he did not begin,
He would surely scuttle his nob,
If he kept him so long in the mob;

Then so loudly began for to sing,
He made the whole church to ring;
Crying, Dolly, my dear, come hither,
And let us be tacked together;
For it is you I intend to wed,
And indulge with the half of my bed,
For the honour of Arthur O'Bradley!
   O! rare Arthur O'Bradley! wonderful Arthur
     O'Bradley!
   Sweet Arthur O'Bradley, O!

Then the vicar his duty discharged,
Without either fee or reward,
Declaring no money he'd have;
And poor Arthur he'd none to give:
So, to make him a little amends,
He invited him home with his friends,
To have a sweet kiss at the bride,
To eat a good dinner beside.
The dishes, though few, were good,
And the sweetest of animal food:
First, a roast guinea-pig and a bantam,
A sheep's head stewed in a lanthorn,
Two calves' feet, and a bull's trotter,
The fore and hind leg of an otter,
With craw-fish, cockles, and crabs,
Lump-fish, limpits, and dabs,
Red herrings and sprats, by dozens,
To feast all their uncles and cousins;
Who seemed well pleased with their treat,

And heartily they did all eat,
For the honour of Arthur O'Bradley!
    O! rare Arthur O'Bradley! wonderful Arthur
        O'Bradley!
    Sweet Arthur O'Bradley, O!

Now, the guests being well satisfied,
The fragments were laid on one side,
When Arthur, to make their hearts merry,
Brought ale, and parkin, and perry;
When Timothy Twig stept in,
With his pipe, and a pipkin of gin.
A lad that was pleasant and jolly,
And scorned to meet melancholy:
He would chaunt and pipe so well,
No youth could him excell.
Not Pan, the god of the swains,
Could ever produce such strains;
But Arthur, being first in the throng,
He swore he would sing the first song,
And one that was pleasant and jolly :
And that should be Hence, Melancholy !
Now give me a dance, quoth Doll,
Come, Jeffery, play up Mad Moll,
'Tis time to be merry and frisky,—
But first I must have some more whiskey;
For I hate your barley swipes,
It does not agree with my tripes,—
It makes me so qualmish and queery.
Oh! you're right, says Arthur, my deary!
My lilly! my lark! and my love!

My daffy-down-dilly! my dove!
My everything! my wife!
I ne'er was so pleased in my life,
Since my name it was Arthur O'Bradley!
   O! rare Arthur O'Bradley! wonderful Arthur
     O'Bradley!
   Sweet Arthur O'Bradley, O!

Then the piper he screwed up his bags,
And the girls began shaking their rags;
First up jumped old Mother Crewe,
Two stockings, and never a shoe.
Her nose was crookèd and long,
Which she could easily lick with her tongue;
And a hump on her back she did not lack,
But you should take no notice of that;
For though threescore years and ten,
She had something was pleasing to men.
And her mouth stood all awry,
And she never was heard to lie,
For she had been dumb from her birth;
So she nodded consent to the mirth,
For honour of Arthur O'Bradley.
   O! rare Arthur O'Bradley! wonderful Arthur
     O'Bradley!
   Sweet Arthur O'Bradley, O!

Then the parson led off at the top,
Some danced, while others did hop;
While some ran foul of the wall,

And others down backwards did fall.
You'd have laughed to see their odd stumps,
False teeth, china eyes, and cork rumps;
While some but one leg they had gotten,
And that which they had it was rotten.
There was lead up and down, figure in,
Four hands across, then back again.
So in dancing they spent the whole night,
Till bright Phœbus appeared in their sight;
When each had a kiss of the bride,
And hopped home to his own fire-side :
Well pleased was Arthur O'Bradley!

   O! rare Arthur O'Bradley! wonderful Arthur
     O'Bradley!
   Sweet Arthur O'Bradley, O!

II.

The Painful Plough.

THIS is one of our oldest agricultural ditties, and maintains its popularity to the present hour. It is called for at merry-makings and feasts in
every part of the country. The tune is in the minor key, and of
a pleasing character.

COME, all you jolly ploughmen, of courage stout and bold,
That labour all the winter in stormy winds, and cold ;
To cloath the fields with plenty, your farm-yards to renew,
To crown them with contentment, behold the painful plough!

Hold ! ploughman, said the gardener, don't count your trade
    with ours,
Walk through the garden, and view the early flowers;
Also the curious border and pleasant walks go view,—
There's none such peace and plenty performèd by the plough!

Hold! gardener, said the ploughman, my calling don't despise,
Each man for his living upon his trade relies ;
Were it not for the ploughman, both rich and poor would rue,
For we are all dependant upon the painful plough.

Adam in the garden was sent to keep it right,
But the length of time he stayed there, I believe it was
    one night;
Yet of his own labour, I call it not his due,
Soon he lost his garden, and went to hold the plough.

For Adam was a ploughman when ploughing first begun,
The next that did succeed him was Cain, the eldest son ;
Some of the generation this calling now pursue;
That bread may not be wanting, remains the painful plough.

Sampson was the strongest man, and Solomon was wise,
Alexander for to conquer 'twas all his daily prise ;
King David was valiant, and many thousands slew,
Yet none of these brave heroes could live without the plough!

Behold the wealthy merchant, that trades in foreign seas,
And brings home gold and treasure for those who live at ease;
With fine silks and spices, and fruits also, too,
They are brought from the Indies by virtue of the plough.

Yes! the man that brings them will own to what is true,
He cannot sail the ocean without the painful plough! [peas,
For they must have bread, biscuit, rice-pudding, flour and
To feed the jolly sailors as they sail o'er the seas.

I hope there's none offended at me for singing this,
For it is not intended for any thing amiss;
If you consider rightly, you'll find what I say is true,
For all that you can mention depends upon the plough.

III.

The Useful Plow; or, The Plowman's Praise.

THE common editions of this popular song say, "From an Old
Ballad." The editor has not been able to meet with the original.

A COUNTRY life is sweet!
In moderate cold and heat,
    To walk in the air,
    How pleasant and fair!
In every field of wheat,
    The fairest of flowers
    Adorning the bowers,
And every meadow now;
    To that, I say,
    No courtier may
    Compare with they
    Who clothe in grey,
And follow the useful plow.

They rise with the morning lark,
And labour till almost dark ;
   Then folding their sheep,
   They hasten to sleep;
While every pleasant park,
   Next morning is ringing,
   With birds that are singing,
On each green, tender bough.
   With what content,
   And merriment,
   Their days are spent,
   Whose minds are bent
To follow the useful plow.

The gallant that dresses fine,
And drinks his bottles of wine,
   Were he to be tried,
   His feathers of pride,
Which deck and adorn his back,
   Are taylors and mercers,
   And other men dressers,
For which they do dun them now.
   But Ralph and Will
   No compters fill
   For taylor's bill,
   Or garments still,
But follow the useful plow.

Their hundreds, without remorse,
Some spend to keep dogs and horse,

Who never would give,
As long as they live,
Not two-pence to help the poor :
Their wives are neglected,
And harlots respected ;
This grieves the nation now ;
But 'tis not so,
With us that go
Where pleasures flow,
To reap and mow,
And follow the useful plow.

———

IV.

The Farmer's Son.

FROM *The British Musical Miscellany ; or, the Delightful Grove ;* a
work published about 1796. The song is old, and often heard
in the dales of Yorkshire.

———

SWEET Nelly! my heart's delight!
Be loving, and do not slight
The proffer I make, for modesty's sake,—
I honour your beauty bright.
For love, I profess, I can do no less,
Thou hast my favour won:
And since I see your modesty,
I pray agree, and fancy me,
Though I'm but a farmer's son.

No! I am a lady gay,
'Tis very well known I may

Have men of renown, in country or town;
  So! Roger, without delay,
Court Bridget or Sue, Kate, Nancy, or Prue,
  Their loves will soon be won;
But don't you dare to speak me fair,
As if I were at my last prayer,
  To marry a farmer's son.

My father has riches' store,
  Two hundred a year, and more;
Beside sheep and cows, carts, harrows, and ploughs;
  His age is above threescore.
And when he does die, then merrily I
  Shall have what he has won;
Both land and kine, all shall be thine,
If thou'lt incline, and wilt be mine,
  And marry a farmer's son.

A fig for your cattle and corn!
  Your proffered love I scorn!
'Tis known very well, my name is Nell,
  And you're but a bumpkin born.
Well! since it is so, away I will go,—
  And I hope no harm is done;
Farewell, adieu!—I hope to woo
As good as you,—and win her, too,
  Though I'm but a farmer's son.

Be not in such haste, quoth she,
  Perhaps we may still agree;

For, man, I protest I was but in jest!
  Come, prythee sit down by me;
For thou art the man that verily can
  Win me, if e'er I'm won;
Both straight and tall, genteel withall,
Therefore, I shall be at your call,
  To marry a farmer's son.

  Dear lady! believe me now
  I solemnly swear and vow,
No lords in their lives take pleasure in wives,
  Like fellows that drive the plough:
For whatever they gain with labour and pain,
  They don't with't to harlots run,
As courtiers do.   I never knew
A London beau that could out-do
  A country farmer's son.

———

V.

Wooing Song of a Yeoman of Kent's Sonne.

THERE are modern copies of this song, but the present version
is copied from *Melismata, Musical phansies fitting the court, citie,
and countree.   To 3, 4, and 5 voyces.   London, printed by William
Stansby, for Thomas Adams,* 1611.

———

I HAVE house and land in Kent,
  And if you'll love me, love me now;
Two-pence half-penny is my rent,—
  I cannot come every day to woo.
Chorus. Two-pence half-penny is his rent,
      And he cannot come every day to woo.

Ich am my vather's eldest zonne,
  My mother eke doth love me well!
For I can bravely clout my shoone,
  And Ich full well can ring a bell.
Cho.   For he can bravely clout his shoone,
    And he full well can ring a bell.

My vather he gave me a hogge,
  My mouther she gave me a zow;
I have a god-vather dwels there by,
  And he on me bestowed a plow.
Cho.   He has a god-vather dwels there by,
    And he on him bestowed a plow.

One time I gave thee a paper of pins,
  Anoder time a taudry lace;
And if thou wilt not grant me love,
  In truth I die bevore thy vace.
Cho.   And if thou wilt not grant his love,
    In truth he'll die bevore thy vace.

Ich have been twice our Whitson Lord,
  Ich have had ladies many vare;
And eke thou hast my heart in hold,
  And in my minde zeemes passing rare.
Cho.   And eke thou hast his heart in hold,
    And in his minde zeemes passing rare.

Ich will put on my best white sloppe,
  And ich will weare my yellow hose;

And on my head a good gray hat,
   And in't ich sticke a lovely rose.
Cho.   And on his head a good gray hat,
     And in't he'll stick a lovely rose.

Wherefore cease off, make no delay,
   And if you'll love me, love me now;
Or els ich zeeke zome oder where,—
   For Ich cannot come every day to woo.
Cho.   Or else he'll zeeke zome oder where,
     For he cannot come every day to woo.

VI.

Harvest-Home Song.

OUR copy of this song is taken from one in the Roxburgh Collection, where it is called, *The Country Farmer's vain glory; in a new song of Harvest Home, sung to a new tune much in request. Licensed according to order.*

OUR oats they are howed, and our barley's reaped,
Our hay is mowed, and our hovels heaped;
   Harvest home! harvest home!
We'll merrily roar out our harvest home!
   Harvest home! harvest home!
We'll merrily roar out our harvest home!
We'll merrily roar out our harvest home!

We cheated the parson, we'll cheat him again;
For why should the vicar have one in ten?
   One in ten! one in ten!

For why should the vicar have one in ten?
For why should the vicar have one in ten?
For staying while dinner is cold and hot,
And pudding and dumpling's burnt to pot;
     Burnt to pot! burnt to pot!
Till pudding and dumpling's burnt to pot,
     Burnt to pot! burnt to pot!

We'll drink off the liquor while we can stand,
And hey for the honour of old England!
     Old England! old England!
And hey for the honour of old England!
     Old England! old England!

Printed for P. Brooksby, J. Dencon, [Deacon]. J. Blai[r], and
J. Back.

VII.

Harvest Home.

From an old copy without printer's name or date.

     COME, Roger and Nell,
     Come, Simpkin and Bell,
  Each lad with his lass hither come;
     With singing and dancing,
     And pleasure advancing,
  To celebrate harvest-home!
Chorus.   'Tis Ceres bids play,
     And keep holiday,

To celebrate harvest-home!
　Harvest-home!
　Harvest-home!
To celebrate harvest-home!

　Our labour is o'er,
　Our barns, in full store,
Now swell with rich gifts of the land;
　Let each man then take,
　For the prong and the rake,
His can and his lass in his hand.
For Ceres, &c.

　No courtier can be
　So happy as we,
In innocence, pastime, and mirth.
　While thus we carouse,
　With our sweetheart or spouse,
And rejoice o'er the fruits of the earth.
For Ceres, &c.

VIII.

The Mow.

A HARVEST HOME SONG.

Tune, " Where the bee sucks."

THIS favourite song, copied from a chap-book called *The Whistling Ploughman*, published at the commencement of the present century, is written in imitation of Ariel's song, in the *Tempest*. It is probably taken from some defunct ballad-opera.

N

Now our work's done, thus we feast,
After labour comes our rest;
Joy shall reign in every breast,
And right welcome is each guest:
     After harvest merrily,
Merrily, merrily, will we sing now,
After the harvest that heaps up the mow.

Now the plowman he shall plow,
And shall whistle as he go,
Whether it be fair or blow,
For another barley mow,
     O'er the furrow merrily:
Merrily, merrily, will we sing now,
After the harvest, the fruit of the plow.

Toil and plenty, toil and ease,
Still the husbandman he sees;
Whether when the winter freeze,
Or in summer's gentle breeze;
     Still he labours merrily,
Merrily, merrily, after the plow,
He looks to the harvest, that gives us the mow.

IX.

The Barley-Mow Song.

THIS song is sung at country meetings in Devon and Cornwall, particularly on completing the carrying of the barley, when the rick, or mow of barley, is finished. On putting up the last sheaf, which is called the craw, (or crow) sheaf, the man who has it cries out "I have it, I have it, I have it;" another says, "What have'ee, what have'ee, what have'ee?" The answer is, "A craw! a craw! a craw!" there is then some cheering, &c., and a supper afterwards. The effect of the barley-mow song cannot be given in words, it should be heard, to appreciate it properly, — particularly with the West-country dialect.

———

HERE's a health to the barley-mow, my brave boys,
   Here's a health to the barley-mow !
We'll drink it out of the jolly brown bowl,
   Here's a health to the barley-mow!
Cho. Here's a health to the barley-mow, my brave boys,
      Here's a health to the barley-mow!

We'll drink it out of the nipperkin, boys,
   Here's a health to the barley-mow!
The nipperkin ar d the jolly brown bowl,
      Cho. Here's a health, &c.

We'll drink it out of the quarter-pint, boys,
   Here's a health to the barley-mow!
The quarter-pint, nipperkin, &c.
      Cho. Here's a health, &c.

We'll drink it out of the half-a-pint, boys,
   Here's a health to the barley-mow!
The half-a-pint, quarter-pint, &c.
      Cho. Here's a health, &c.

We'll drink it out of the pint, my brave boys,
   Here's a health to the barley-mow!
The pint, the half-a-pint, &c.
        Cho.   Here's a health, &c.

We'll drink it out of the quart, my brave boys,
   Here's a health to the barley-mow!
The quart, the pint, &c.
        Cho.   Here's a health, &c.

We'll drink it out of the pottle, my boys,
   Here's a health to the barley-mow!
The pottle, the quart, &c.
        Cho.   Here's a health, &c.

We'll drink it out of the gallon, my boys,
      Here's a health to the barley-mow!
The gallon, the pottle, &c.
        Cho.   Here's a health, &c.

We'll drink it out of the half-anker, boys,
   Here's a health to the barley-mow!
The half-anker, gallon, &c.
        Cho.   Here's a health, &c.

We'll drink it out of the anker, my boys,
   Here's a health to the barley mow!
The anker, the half-anker, &c.
        Cho.   Here's a health, &c.

We'll drink it out of the half-hogshead, boys,
   Here's a health to the barley-mow!

The half-hogshead, anker, &c.
> *Cho.*   Here's a health, &c.

We'll drink it out of the hogshead, my boys,
  Here's a health to the barley-mow!
The hogshead, the half-hogshead, &c.
> *Cho.*   Here's a health, &c.

We'll drink it out of the pipe, my brave boys,
  Here's a health to the barley-mow!
The pipe, the hogshead, &c.
> *Cho.*   Here's a health, &c.

We'll drink it out of the well, my brave boys,
  Here's a health to the barley mow!
The well, the pipe, &c.
> *Cho.*   Here's a health, &c.

We'll drink it out of the river, my boys,
  Here's a health to the barley-mow!
The river, the well, &c.
> *Cho.*   Here's a health, &c.

We'll drink it out of the ocean, my boys,
  Here's a health to the barley-mow!
The ocean, the river, the well, the pipe, the hogshead,
      the half-hogshead, the anker, the half-anker,
      the gallon, the pottle, the quart, the pint, the
      half-a-pint, the quarter-pint, the nipperkin, and
      the jolly brown bowl!

Cho. Here's a health to the barley-mow, my brave boys!
Here's a health to the barley-mow!

————

The above verses are very much *ad libitum*, but always in the
third line repeating the whole of the previously named mea-
sures; and, as the last verse is sometimes the ocean, we have
concluded with it at length.

————

X.

The Craven Churn-Supper Song.

IN some of the more remote dales of Craven it is customary at
the close of the hay-harvest for the farmers to give an entertainment to their men; this is called the churn supper; a name which
Eugene Aram says has its origin because it " has been from im-
memorial times, customary to produce at such suppers a great
quantity of cream in a churn, and to circulate it in cups to each
of the rustic company, to be eaten with bread." At these churn-
suppers the masters and their families attend the entertainment,
and share in the general mirth. The men on these occasions mask
themselves, and dress in a grotesque manner, and are allowed the
privilege of playing harmless practical jokes on their employers,
&c. The churn-supper song varies in different dales, but the
following used to be the most popular version. In the third
verse there seems to be an allusion to the clergyman's taking
tythe in kind, on which occasions it is customary for him to be
accompanied by two or three men, and the parish clerk. The
song has never before been printed.

————

GOD rest you, merry gentlemen!
Be not movèd at my strain,
For nothing study shall my brain,
But for to make you laugh.
For I came here to this feast,

For to laugh, carouse, and jest,
And welcome shall be every guest,
  To drink his cup and can.
Chorus. Be frolicksome, every one,
        Melancholy none ;
        Drink about!
        See it out,
        And then we'll all go home,
        And then we'll all go home!

This ale it is a gallant thing,
It cheers the spirits of a king ;
It makes a dumb man strive to sing,
  Aye, and a beggar play!
A cripple that is lame and halt,
And scarce a mile a day can walk,
When he feels the juice of malt,
  Will throw his crutch away.
Cho. Be frolicksome, &c.

'Twill make the parson forget his men,—
'Twill make his clerk forget his pen ;
'Twill turn a tailor's giddy brain,
  And make him break his wand.
The blacksmith loves it as his life,—
It make the tinkler bang his wife,—
Aye, and the butcher seek his knife,
  When he has it in his hand!
Cho. Be frolicksome, &c.

So now to conclude, my merry boys, all,
Let's with strong liquor take a fall,

Although the weakest goes to the wall,
 The best is but a play!
For water it concludes in noise,
Good ale will chear our hearts, brave boys,
Then put it round with a cheerful voice,
 We meet not every day.
 Cho. Be frolicksome, &c.

———

XI.

The Rural Dance about the May-Pole.

THE most correct copy of this song is the one in *The Westminster Drollery*, Part II. p. 80. It is there called *The Rural Dance about the May-pole, the tune, the first-figure dance at Mr. Young's ball, May* 1671. The tune may be found in Chappell's *National English Airs.* The last verse in our copy is modern, and, we believe, was written by a comic song-writer, who, a few years ago, had the impudence to palm the whole song off, on those who knew no better, as his own composition.

———

COME, lasses and lads,
Take leave of your dads,
 And away to the may-pole hie;
For every he
Has got him a she,
 And the minstrel 's standing by.
For Willie has gotten his Jill,
 And Johnny has got his Joan,
To jig it, jig it, jig it,
 Jig it up and down.

Strike up, says Wat,
Agreed, says Kate,
   And I prithee, fiddler, play;
Content, says Hodge,
And so says Madge,
   For this is a holiday.
Then every man did put
   His hat off to his lass,
And every girl did curchy,
   Curchy, curchy on the grass.

Begin, says Hall,
Aye, aye, says Mall,
   We'll lead up *Packington's Pound:*
No, no, says Noll,
And so says Doll,
   We'll first have *Sellenger's Round.*
Then every man began
   To foot it round about;
And every girl did jet it,
   Jet it, jet it, in and out.

You're out, says Dick,
'Tis a lie, says Nick,
   The fiddler played it false;
'Tis true, says Hugh,
And so says Sue,
   And so says nimble Alice.
The fiddler then began
   To play the tune again,

And every girl did trip it, trip it,
Trip it to the men.

Let's kiss, says Jane,
Content, says Nan,
    And so says every she;
How many? says Batt,
Why three, says Matt,
    For that's a maiden's fee.
But they, instead of three,
    Did give them half a score,
And they in kindness gave 'em, gave 'em,
    Gave 'em as many more.

Then after an hour,
They went to a bower,
    And played for ale and cakes;
And kisses, too;—
Until they were due,
    The lasses kept the stakes:
The girls did then begin
    To quarrel with the men;
And bid 'em take their kisses back,
    And give them their own again.

Yet there they sate,
Until it was late,
    And tired the fiddler quite,
With singing and playing,
Without any paying,
    From morning unto night:

They told the fiddler then,
　　They'd pay him for his play;
And each a two-pence, two-pence,
　　Gave him, and went away.

[Good night, says Harry,
Good night, says Mary,
　　Good night, says Dolly to John;
Good night, says Sue,
Good night, says Hugh;
　　Good night, says every one.
Some walked, and some did run,
　　Some loitered on the way; [love-knots,
And bound themselves with love-knots,
　　To meet the next holiday.]

———

XII.

The Helstone Furry-day Song.

At Helstone in Cornwall, the 8th of May is a day devoted to revelry
and gaiety. It is called the Furry-day, supposed to be a corrup-
tion of Flora's day, from the garlands worn and carried in proces-
sion during the festival. A writer in the *Gentleman's Magazine* for
June 1790, says, " In the morning, very early, some troublesome
rogues go round the streets [of Helstone], with drums, and
other noisy instruments, disturbing their sober neighbours, and
singing parts of a song, the whole of which nobody now recol-
lects, and of which I know no more than that there is mention
in it of the " grey goose quill," and of going " to the green wood"
to bring home " the Summer and the May, O!" During the
festival, the gentry, tradespeople, servants, &c., dance through

the streets, and thread through certain of the houses to a very old dance tune, given in the appendix to Davies Gilbert's *Christmas Carols*, and which may also be found in Chappell's *National English Airs*, and other popular collections. The Furry-day song possesses no literary merit whatever; but as a part of an old, and really interesting festival, it is worthy of preservation. The dance-tune has been confounded with that of the song, but Mr. Sandys, to whom the editor is indebted for this communication, observes "the dance-tune is quite different."

———

Robin Hood and Little John,
  They both are gone to the fair, O!
And we will go to the merry green-wood,
  To see what they do there, O!
    And for to chase, O!
  To chase the buck and doe.
      With ha-lan-tow, rumble, O!
      For we were up as soon as any day, O!
      And for to fetch the summer home,
      The summer and the may, O!
      For summer is a-come, O!
      And winter is a-gone, O!

Where are those Spaniards
  That make so great a boast, O?
They shall eat the grey goose feather,
  And we will eat the roast, O!
    In every land, O!
  The land where'er we go.
      With ha-lan-tow, &c.

As for St. George, O!
  Saint George he was a knight, O!
Of all the knights in Christendom,
  Saint Georgy is the right, O!
    In every land, O!
    The land where'er we go.
      With ha-lan-tow, &c.

XIII.

Cornish Midsummer Bonfire Song.

THE very ancient custom of lighting fires on Midsummer-eve, being the vigil of St. John the Baptist, is still kept up in several parts of Cornwall. On these occasions the fishermen and others dance about them, and sing appropriate songs. The following has been sung for a long series of years at Penzance and the neighbourhood, and is taken down from the recitation of a leader of a West-country choir. It is communicated to our pages by Mr. Sandys. The origin of the Midsummer bonfires is fully entered upon in Brand's *Popular Antiquities.*—Vide Sir H. Ellis's edition of that work, vol. i. pp. 166-186.

THE bonny month of June is crowned
  With the sweet scarlet rose;
The groves and meadows all around
  With lovely pleasure flows.

As I walked out to yonder green,
  One evening so fair;
All where the fair maids may be seen
  Playing at the bonfire.

Hail! lovely nymphs, be not too coy,
　　But freely yield your charms;
Let love inspire with mirth and joy,
　　In Cupid's lovely arms.

Bright Luna spreads its light around,
　　The gallants for to cheer;
As they lay sporting on the ground,
　　At the fair June bonfire.

All on the pleasant dewy mead,
　　They shared each other's charms;
Till Phœbus' beams began to spread,
　　And coming day alarms.

Whilst larks and linnets sing so sweet,
　　To cheer each lovely swain;
Let each prove true unto their love,
　　And so farewell the plain.

XIV.

Suffolk Harvest-Home Song.

In no part of England are the harvest-homes kept up with greater
spirit than in Suffolk. The following old song is a general
favourite on such occasions.

Here's a health unto our master,
　　The founder of the feast!
I wish, with all my heart and soul,
　　In heaven he may find rest.

I hope all things may prosper,
　　That ever he takes in hand;
For we are all his servants,
　　And all at his command.
Drink, boys, drink, and see you do not spill,
　For if you do, you must drink two,—it is your
　　　master's will.

Now our harvest is ended,
　　And supper is past;
Here's our mistress' good health,
　　In a full flowing glass!
She is a good woman, —
　　She prepared us good cheer;
Come, all my brave boys,
　　And drink off your beer.
Drink, my boys, drink 'till you come unto me,
The longer we sit, my boys, the merrier shall we be!

In yon green wood there lies an old fox,
Close by his den you may catch him, or no;
Ten thousand to one you catch him, or no.
His beard and his brush are all of one colour,—

　　　[*Takes the glass, and empties it off.*]

I am sorry, kind sir, that your glass is no fuller.
'Tis down the red lane! 'tis down the red lane!
So merrily hunt the fox down the red lane!

XV.

The Haymakers' Song.

An old and very favourite ditty sung in many parts of England
at merry-makings, especially at those which occur during the
hay-harvest.   It is not in any collection.

————

In the merry month of June,
    In the prime time of the year;
Down in yonder meadows
    There runs a river clear :
And many a little fish
    Doth in that river play;
And many a lad, and many a lass,
    Go abroad a-making hay.

In come the jolly mowers,
    To mow the meadows down;
With budget, and with bottle
    Of ale, both stout and brown,
All labouring men of courage bold
    Come here their strength to try;
They sweat and blow, and cut and mow,
    For the grass cuts very dry.

Here's nimble Ben and Tom,
    With pitchfork, and with rake;
Here's Molly, Liz and Susan,
    Come here their hay to make.
While sweet jug, jug, jug!
    The nightingale doth sing,

From morning unto even-song,
　As they are hay-making.

And when that bright day faded,
　And the sun was going down,
There was a merry piper
　Approached from the town :
He pulled out his pipe and tabor,
　So sweetly he did play,
Which made all lay down their rakes,
　And leave off making hay.

Then joining in a dance,
　They jig it o'er the green;
Though tired with their labour,
　No one less was seen.
But sporting like some fairies,
　Their dance they did pursue,
In leading up, and casting off,
　Till morning was in view.*

And when that bright daylight,
　The morning it was come,
They laid down and rested
　Till the rising of the sun :
Till the rising of the sun,
　When the merry larks do sing,
And each lad did rise and take his lass,
　And away to hay-making.

XVI.

The Sword-Dancers' Song.

SWORD-DANCING is not so common in the North of England as it was a few years ago; but a troop of rustic practitioners of the art may still be occasionally met with at Christmas time, in some of the most secluded of the Yorkshire dales.   The following is a copy of the introductory song, as it used to be sung by the Wharfdale sword-dancers.   It was transcribed by the editor from a MS. in possession of Mr. Holmes, surgeon, at Grassington, in Craven.   At the conclusion of the song a dance ensues, and sometimes a rustic drama is performed, similar to the one given in an article on sword-dancing, to be found in Sir Cuthbert Sharp's *Bishoprick Garland.*

———

The spectators being assembled, the clown enters, and after drawing a circle with his sword, walks round it, and calls in the
actors in the following lines, which are sung to the accompaniment of a violin played outside, or behind the door.

———

THE first that enters on the floor,
    His name is Captain Brown ;
I think he is as smart a youth
    As any in this town:
In courting of the ladies gay,
    He fixes his delight;
He will not stay from them all day,
    And is with them all the night.

The next 's a tailor by his trade,
    Called Obadiah Trim;
You may quickly guess, by his plain dress,
    And hat of broadest brim,

That he is of the Quaking sect,
   Who would seem to act by merit
Of yeas and nays, and hums and hahs,
   And motions of the spirit.

The next that enters on the floor,
   He is a foppish knight;
The first to be in modish dress,
   He studies day and night.
Observe his habit round about,—
   Even from top to toe;
The fashion late from France was brought,—
   He's finer than a beau!

Next I present unto your view
   A very worthy man;
He is a vintner, by his trade,
   And Love-ale is his name.
If gentlemen propose a glass,
   He seldom says 'em nay,
But does always think it's right to drink,
   While other people pay.

The next that enters on the floor,
   It is my beauteous dame;
Most dearly I do her adore,
   And Bridget is her name.
At needlework she does excell
   All that e'er learnt to sew,
And when I choose, she'll ne'er refuse,
   What I command her do.

And I myself am come long since,
　　And Thomas is my name;
Though some are pleased to call me Tom,
　　I think they're much to blame :
Folks should not use their betters thus,
　　But I value it not a groat,
Though the tailors, too, that botching crew,
　　Have patched it on my coat.

I pray who's this we've met with here,
　　That tickles his trunk weam ?
We've picked him up as here we came,
　　And cannot learn his name:
But sooner than he's go without,
　　I'll call him my son Tom;
And if he'll play, be it night or day,
　　We'll dance you *Jumping Joan.*

XVII.

The Maskers' Song.

In the Yorkshire dales the young men are in the habit of going
about at Christmas time in grotesque masks, and of performing
in the farm-houses a sort of rude drama, accompanied by singing
and music. The maskers have wooden swords, and the per-
formance is an evening one. The following version of their
introductory song was taken down by the editor from the recitation of a young besom-maker, now residing at Linton, in Craven,
and who for some years past, has been one of these rustic
actors. From the mention of the pace, or paschal-egg, it is

evident that the play was originally an Easter pageant, which, in consequence of the decline of the gorgeous rites formerly connected with that festival, has been transferred to Christmas, the only season which, in the rural districts of Protestant England, is observed after the olden fashion. The maskers generally consist of five characters, one of whom officiates in the three-fold capacity of clown, fiddler, and master of the ceremonies.

Enter clown, who sings in a sort of chaunt, or recitative,

> I OPEN this door, I enter in,
> I hope your favour for to win;
> Whether we shall stand or fall,
> We do endeavour to please you all.

> A room! a room! a gallant room,
>   A room to let us ride!
> We are not of the raggald sort,
>   But of the royal tribe:
> Stir up the fire, and make a light,
> To see the bloody act to-night!

[Here another of the party introduces his companions by singing to a violin accompaniment, as follows:]

> Here's two or three jolly boys,
>   All in one mind;
> We've come a pace-egging,—
>   I hope you'll prove kind:
> I hope you'll prove kind
>   With your money and beer,
> We shall come no more near you
>   Until the next year.
>   Fal de ral, lal de lal, &c.

The first that steps up
   Is Lord [Nelson] you'll see,
With a bunch of blue ribbons
   Tied down to his knee;
With a star on his breast,
   Like silver doth shine;
I hope you'll remember
   This pace-egging time.
       Fal de ral, &c.

O! the next that steps up
   Is a jolly Jack tar,
He sailed with Lord [Nelson],
   In during last war:
He's a right on the sea,
   Old England to view:
He's come a pace-egging
   With so jolly a crew.
       Fal de ral, &c.

O! the next that steps up
   Is old Toss-Pot, you'll see,
He's a valiant old man,
   In every degree.
He's a valiant old man,
   And he wears a pig-tail;
And all his delight
   Is drinking mulled ale.
       Fal de ral, &c.

O! the next that steps up
  Is old Miser, you'll see;
She heaps up her white
  And her yellow money;
She wears her old rags
  Till she starves and she begs;
And she's come here to ask
  For a dish of pace-eggs.
    Fal de ral, &c.

[The characters being thus duly introduced, the following lines
are sung in chorus by all the party.]

Gentlemen and ladies, that sit by the fire,
Put your hand in your pocket, 'tis all we desire;
Put your hand in your pocket, and pull out your purse,
And give us a trifle,—you'll not be much worse.

[Here follows a dance, and this is generally succeeded by a dialogue of an *ad libitum* character, and which varies in different
districts, being sometimes similar to the one performed by the
sword-dancers.]

* * *

XVIII.

Gloucestershire Wassailers' Song.

It is still customary in many parts of England to hand round
the wassail, or health-bowl, on New-Year's Eve. The custom is
supposed to be of Saxon origin, and to be derived from one of
the observances of the Feast of Yule.

* * *

Wassail! wassail! all over the town,
Our toast it is white, and our ale it is brown;

Our bowl is made of a maplin tree;
We be good fellows all;—I drink to thee.

Here's to our horse, and to his right ear,
God send our measter a happy new year;
A happy new year as e'er he did see,—
With my wassailing bowl I drink to thee.

Here's to our mare, and to her right eye,
God send our mistress a good Christmas pie;
A good Christmas pie as e'er I did see,—
With my wassailing bowl I drink to thee.

Here's to our cow, and to her long tail,
God send our measter us never may fail
Of a cup of good beer: I pray you draw near,
And our jolly wassail it's then you shall hear.

Be here any maids? I suppose there be some;
Sure they will not let young men stand on the cold stone!
Sing hey O, maids! come trole back the pin,
And the fairest maid in the house let us all in.

Come, butler, come, bring us a bowl of the best;
I hope your soul in heaven will rest;
But if you do bring us a bowl of the small,
Then down fall butler, and bowl and all.

———

XIX.

Richard of Taunton Dean ; or Dumble dum deary.

This song is very popular with the country-people in every part of England, but more particularly so with the inhabitants of the counties of Somerset, Devon, and Cornwall.   There are many different versions.   The following one, communicated by Mr. Sandys, was taken down from the singing of an old blind fiddler, "who," says Mr. Sandys, " used to accompany it on his instrument in an original and humorous manner; a representative of the old minstrels!"

———

Last New-Year's day, as I've heerd say,
Young Richard he mounted his dapple grey,
And he trotted along to Taunton Dean,
To court the parson's daughter, Jean.
     Dumble dum deary, dumble dum deary,
     Dumble dum deary, dumble dum dee.

With buckskin breeches, shoes and hose,
And Dicky put on his Sunday clothes;
Likewise a hat upon his head,
All bedaubed with ribbons red.

Young Richard he rode without dread or fear,
Till he came to the house where lived his sweet dear,
When he knocked, and shouted, and bellowed, hallo !
Be the folks at home ? say aye or no.

A trusty servant let him in,
That he his courtship might begin;

Young Richard he walked along the great hall,
And loudly for mistress Jean did call.

Miss Jean she came without delay,
To hear what Dicky had got to say;
I s'pose you knaw me, mistress Jean,
I'm honest Richard of Taunton Dean.

I'm an honest fellow, although I be poor,
And I never was in love afore;
My mother she bid me come here for to woo,
And I can fancy none but you.

Suppose that I would be your bride,
Pray how would you for me provide?
For I can neither sew nor spin,—
Pray what will your day's work bring in?

Why, I can plough, and I can zow,
And zometimes to the market go
With Gaffer Johnson's straw or hay,
And yarn my ninepence every day!

Ninepence a-day will never do,
For I must have silks and satins too!
Ninepence a day won't buy us meat!
Adzooks! says Dick, I've a zack of wheat;

Besides, I have a house hard by,
'Tis all my awn, when mammy do die;
If thee and I were married now,
Ods! I'd feed thee as fat as my feyther's old zow.

Dick's compliments did so delight,
They made the family laugh outright;
Young Richard took huff, and no more would say,
He kicked up old Dobbin and trotted away,
Singing, dumble dum deary, &c.

XX.

As Tom was a-walking.

AN ANCIENT CORNISH SONG.

THIS song, said to be translated from the Cornish, "was taken
down," says Mr. Sandys, "from the recital of a modern Cory-
pheus, or leader of a parish choir, who said the *antiquity* of it
was very *auncient !*"

As Tom was a-walking one fine summer's morn,
When the dazies and gold cups the fields did adorn;
He met cozen Mal, with the tub on her head,
Says Tom, Cozen Mal, you might speak if you we'd.

But Mal stamped along, and appeared to be shy,
And Tom singed out, Zounds! I'll knaw of the why?
So back he tore after, in a terrible fuss,
And axed cozen Mal, What's the reason of this?

Tom Treloar, cried out Mal, I'll nothing do wi' 'ee,
Go to Fanny Trembaa, she do knaw how I'm shy;
Tom, this here t'other day, down the hill thee didst stap,
And dab'd a great doat fig in Fan Trembaa's lap.

As for Fanny Trembaa, I ne'er taalked with her twice,
And gived her a doat fig, they are so very nice;

So I'll tell thee, I went to the market t'other day,
And the doat figs I boft, why I saved them away.

Says Mal, Tom Treloar, if that be the caase,
May the Lord bless for ever that sweet pretty faace;
If thee'st give me thy doat figs thee'st boft in the fear,
I'll swear to the now, thee shu'st marry me here.

XXI.

The Miller and his Sons.

A MILLER, especially if he happen to be the owner of a soke-
mill, has always been deemed fair game for the village satirist.
Of the numerous songs written in ridicule of the calling of the
" rogues in grain," the following is one of the best and mᵒ
popular: its quaint humour will recommend it to our readerˢ

THERE was a crafty miller, and he
Had lusty sons, one, two, and three :
He called them all, and asked their will,
If that to them he left his mill.

He called first to his eldest son,
Saying, My life is almost run;
If I to you this mill do make,
What toll do you intend to take?

Father, said he, my name is Jack;
Out of a bushel I'll take a peck,
From every bushel that I grind,
That I may a good living find.

Thou art a fool! the old man said,
Thou hast not well learned thy trade;
This mill to thee I ne'er will give,
For by such toll no man can live.

He called for his middlemost son,
Saying, My life is almost run;
If I to you this mill do make,
What toll do you intend to take?

Father, says he, my mind is Ralph
Out of a bushel I'll take a half,
From every bushel that I grind,
That I may a good living find.

Thou art a fool! the old man said,
Thou hast not well learned thy trade;
This mill to thee I ne'er will give,
For by such toll no man can liv.e.

He called for his youngest son,
Saying, My life is almost run;
If I to you this mill do make,
What toll do you intend to take?

Father, said he, I'm your only boy,
For taking toll is all my joy!
Before I will a good living lack,
I'll take it all, and forswear the sack!

Thou art my boy! the old man said,
For thou hast right well learned thy trade;

This mill to thee I give, he cried,
And then he closed up his eyes and died.

———

XXII.

Joan's Ale was New.

OUR's is the common verson of this popular song; it varies considerably from the one given by D'Urfey in the *Pills to purge Melancholy.* From the names of Nolly and Joan, and the allusion to ale, we are inclined to regard the song as a lampoon levelled at Cromwell and his wife, whom the Royalist party nick-named "Joan." The writer seems to represent the Protector's acquaint‌ances, (who are held up as low and vulgar tradesmen), as paying him a congratulatory visit on his change of fortune, and regaling themselves with the "Brewer's" ale.

———

THERE were six jovial tradesmen,
    And they all sat down to drinking,
    For they were a jovial crew;
They sat themselves down to be merry;
And they called for a bottle of sherry,
You're welcome as the hills, says Nolly,
        While Joan's ale is new, brave boys,
        While Joan's ale is new.

The first that came in was a soldier,
With his firelock over his shoulder,
Sure no one could be bolder,
    And a long broad-sword he drew:

He swore he would fight for England's ground,
Before the nation should be run down,
He boldly drank their healths all round,
    While Joan's ale was new.

The next that came in was a hatter,
Sure no one could be blacker,
And he began to chatter,
    Among the jovial crew:
He threw his hat upon the ground,
And swore every man should spend his pound,
And boldly drank their healths all round,
    While Joan's ale was new.

The next that came in was a dyer,
And he sat himself down by the fire,
For it was his heart's desire
    To drink with the jovial crew:
He told the landlord to his face,
The chimney-corner should be his place,
And there he'd sit and dye his face,
    While Joan's ale was new.

The next that came in was a tinker,
And he was no small beer drinker,
And he was no strong ale shrinker,
    Among the jovial crew:
For his brass nails were made of metal,
And he swore he'd go and mend a kettle,
Good heart, how his hammer and nails did rattle,
    When Joan's ale was new!

The next that came in was a taylor,
With his bodkin, shears, and thimble,
He swore he would be nimble
    Among the jovial crew:
They sat and they called for ale so stout,
Till the poor taylor was almost broke,
And was forced to go and pawn his coat,
    While Joan's ale was new.

The next that came in was a ragman,
With his rag-bag over his shoulder,
Sure no one could be bolder
    Among the jovial crew.
They sat and called for pots and glasses,
Till they were all drunk as asses,
And burnt the old ragman's bag to ashes,
    While Joan's ale was new.

XXIII.

The Leathern Bottel.

SOMERSETSHIRE VERSION.

In Chappell's *National English Airs* is a much longer version of *The Leathern Bottèl.* The following copy is the one sung, at the present time, by the country-people in the county of Somerset. It is communicated to our pages by Mr. Sandys.

God above, who rules all things,
Monks and abbots, and beggars and kings,

The ships that in the sea do swim,
The earth, and all that is therein ;
Not forgetting the old cow's hide,
And every thing else in the world beside :
And I wish his soul in heaven may dwell,
Who first invented this leathern bottèl!

Oh! what do you say to the glasses fine?
Oh! they shall have no praise of mine ;
Suppose a gentleman sends his man
To fill them with liquor, as fast as he can,
The man he falls, in coming away,
And sheds the liquor so fine and gay;
But had it been in the leathern bottèl,
And the stopper been in, 'twould all have been well!

Oh! what do you say to the tankard fine?
Oh! it shall have no praise of mine;
Suppose a man and his wife fall out,—
And such things happen sometimes, no doubt,—
They pull and they haul; in the midst of the fray
They shed the liquor so fine and gay ;
But had it been in the leathern bottèl,
And the stopper been in, 'twould all have been well!

Now, when this bottèl it is worn out,
Out of its sides you may cut a clout ;
This you may hang upon a pin,—
'Twill serve to put odd trifles in ;

P

Ink and soap, and candle-ends,
For young beginners have need of such friends.
And I wish his soul in heaven may dwell,
Who first invented the leathern bottèl!

XXIV.

The Farmer's Old Wife.

A SUSSEX WHISTLING SONG.

THIS is a countryman's whistling-song, and the only one of the kind which the editor remembers to have heard. It is very ancient, and a great favourite. The farmer's wife has an adventure somewhat resembling the hero's in the burlesque version of *Don Giovanni.* The tune is *Lilli burlero*, and the song is sung as follows:—the first line of each verse is given as a solo; then the tune is continued by a chorus of whistlers, who whistle that portion of the air which in *Lilli burlero* would be sung to the words, *Lilli burlero bullen a la.* The songster then proceeds with the tune, and sings the whole of the verse through, after which the strain is concluded by the whistlers. The effect of the song, when accompanied by the strong whistles of a tribe of hardy countrymen, is very striking, and cannot be described by the pen. It should be heard.

THERE was an old farmer in Sussex did dwell,

[Chorus of whistlers.]

There was an old farmer in Sussex did dwell,
And he had a bad wife, as many knew well.

[Chorus of whistlers.]

Then Satan came to the old man at the plough,—
One of your family I must have now.

It is not your eldest son that I crave,
But it is your old wife, and she I will have.

O, welcome! good Satan, with all my heart,
I hope you and she will never more part.

Now Satan has got the old wife on his back,
And he lugged her along, like a pedlar's pack.

He trudged away till they came to his hall-gate,
Says he, Here! take in an old Sussex chap's mate!

O! then she did kick the young imps about,—
Says one to the other, Let's try turn her out.

She spied thirteen imps all dancing in chains,
She up with her pattens, and beat out their brains.

She knocked the old Satan against the wall,—
Let's try turn her out, or she'll murder us all.

Now he's bundled her up on his back amain,
And to her old husband he took her again.

I have been a tormentor the whole of my life,
But I ne'er was tormented so as with your wife.

———

XXV.

Old Witchet and his Wife.

This song still retains its popularity in the North of England,
and, when sung with humour, never fails to elicit roars of laughter. A Scotch version may be found in Herd's Collection, 1769,

and also in Cunningham's *Songs of England and Scotland*, London, 1835. The editor cannot give an opinion as to which is the original, but the English set is of unquestionable antiquity. Our copy was obtained from Yorkshire. It has been collated with one printed at the Aldermary press, and preserved in the third volume of the *Roxburgh Collection*. The tune is peculiar to the song.

———

O! I went into the stable, and there for to see,
And there I saw three horses stand, by one, by two,
       and by three;
O! I called to my loving wife, and Anon, kind sir!
       quoth she;
O! what do these three horses here, without the leave
       of me?
Why, you old fool! blind fool! can't you very well see,
These are three milking cows my mother sent to me?
Ods bobs! well done! milking cows with saddles on!
The like was never known!
Old Wichet a cuckold went out, and a cuckold he came
       home!

O! I went into the kitchen, and there for to see,
And there I saw three swords hang, by one, by two,
       and by three;
O! I called to my loving wife, and Anon, kind sir!
       quoth she;
O! what do these three swords do here, without the
       leave of me?
Why you old fool! blind fool! can't you very well see
These are three roasting spits, my mother sent to me?

Ods bobs! well done! roasting spits with scabbards on!
The like was never known!
Old Wichet a cuckold went out, and a cuckold he came
  home!

O! I went into the parlour, and there for to see,
And there I saw three cloaks hang, by one, by two,
    and by three;
O! I called to my loving wife, and Anon, kind sir!
    quoth she;
O! what do these three cloaks do here, without the
    leave of me?
Why you old fool! blind fool! can't you very well see
These are three mantuas my mother sent to me?
Ods bods! well done! mantuas with capes on!
The like was never known!
Old Wichet a cuckold went out, and a cuckold he came
  home!

O! I went into the pantry, and there for to see,
And there I saw three pair of boots, by one, by two,
    and by three;
O! I called to my loving wife, and Anon, kind sir!
    quoth she;
O! what do these three pair of boots here, without the
    leave of me?
Why you old fool! blind fool! can't you very well see
These are three pudding-bags my mother sent to me?
Ods bobs! well done! pudding-bags with spurs on!
The like was never known!

Old Wichet a cuckold went out, and a cuckold he came
        home!

O! I went into the dairy, and there for to see,
And there I saw three hats hang, by one, by two, and
        by three;   [she;
O! I called to my loving wife, and Anon, kind sir! quoth
Pray what do these three hats here, without the leave
        of me?
Why you old fool! blind fool! can't you very well see
These are three skimming-dishes my mother sent to me?
Ods bobs! well done! skimming-dishes with hat-
        bands on!
The like was never known!
Old Wichet a cuckold went out, and a cuckold he came
        home!

O! I went into the chamber, and there for to see,
And there I saw three men in bed, by one, by two,
        and by three;
O! I called to my loving wife, and Anon, kind sir! quoth
        she;
O! what do these three men here, without the leave
        of me?
Why you old fool! blind fool! can't you very well see
They are three milking-maids my mother sent to me?
Ods bobs! well done! milking-maids with beards on!
The like was never known!
Old Wichet a cuckold went out, and a cuckold he came
        home!

XXVI.

The Yorkshire Horse-Dealer.

THIS ludicrous and genuine Yorkshire song, the production of some unknown country minstrel, was very popular a few years ago, owing to the admirable singing of it by Emery. The incidents actually occurred at the close of the last century, and some of the descendants of "Tommy Towers" were resident at Clapham till within a very recent period, and used to take great delight in relating the laughable adventure of their progenitor. Abey Muggins is understood to be a *sobriquet* for a then Clapham innkeeper. The village of Clapham is in the west of Yorkshire, on the high road betwixt Skipton and Kendal.

BANE ta Claapam town-gate lived an oud Yorkshire tike,
Who i' dealing i' horseflesh hed ne'er met his like ;
Twor his pride that i' aw the hard bargains he'd hit,
He'd bit a girt monny, but nivver bin bit.

This oud Tommy Towers, (bi that naam he wor knaan),
Hed an oud carrion tit that wor sheer skin an' baan;
Ta hev killed him for t' curs wad hev bin quite as well,
But 'twor Tommy opinion he'd dee on himsel !

Well! yan Abey Muggins, a neighborin cheat,
Thowt ta diddle oud Tommy wad be a girt treat;
Hee'd a horse, too, 'twor war than oud Tommy's, ye see,
Fort' neet afore that hee'd thowt proper ta dee!

Thinks Abey, t' oud codger 'll nivver smoak t' trick,
I'll swop wi' him my poor deead horse for his wick,

An' if Tommy I nobbut can happen ta trap,
'Twill be a fine feather i' Aberram cap!

Soa to Tommy he goas, an' the question he pops,
Betwin thy horse and mine, prithee, Tommy, what
　　　swops?
What wilt gi' me ta boot? for mine's t' better horse still!
Nout, says Tommy, I'll swop ivven hands, an' ye will.

Abey preaached a lang time about summat ta boot,
Insistin' that his war the liveliest brute;
But Tommy stuck fast where he first had begun,
Till Abey shook hands, and sed, well, Tommy, done!

O! Tommy, sed Abey, I'ze sorry for thee,
I thowt thou'd a hadden mair white i' thy ee;
Good luck's wi' thy bargin, for my horse is deead:
Hey! says Tommy, my lad, soa is min, an it's fleead!

Soa Tommy got t' better of t' bargin, a vast,
An' cam' off wi' a Yorkshireman's triumph at last;
For thof 'twixt deead horses there's not mitch to choose,
Yet Tommy war richer by t' hide an' fower shooes.

XXVII.

Jone o' Greenfield's Ramble.

THE county of Lancaster has always been famed for its admirable *patois* songs; but they are in general the productions of modern authors, and consequently, however popular they may be, are not within the scope of the present work. In the following humorous production we have, however, a composition of the last century. It is the oldest Lancashire song the editor has been able to procure, as well as one of the most popular; and, from its being witty without being vulgar, has ever been a favourite with all classes of society.

———

SAYS Jone to his wife, on a hot summer's day,
I'm resolved i' Grinfilt no lunger to stay;
For I'll go to Owdham os fast os I can,
So fare thee weel, Grinfilt, un fare thee weel, Nan;
    A soger I'll be, un brave Owdham I'll see,
    Un I'll ha'e a battle wi' th' French.

Dear Jone, then said Nan, un hoo bitterly cried,
Wilt' be one o' th' foote, or tha meons to ride?
Odsounds! wench, I'll ride oather ass or a mule,
Ere I'll kewer i' Grinfilt os black as te dule,
    Booath clemmink un starvink, un never a fardink,
    Ecod! it would drive ony mon mad.

Aye, Jone, sin' we coom i' Grinfilt for t' dwell,
We'n had mony a bare meal, I con vara weel tell;
Bare meal! ecod! aye, that I vara weel know,
There's bin two days this wick ot we'n had nowt at o:
    I'm vara near sided, afore I'll abide it,
    I'll feight oather Spanish or French.

Then says my aunt Marget, Ah! Jone, thee'rt so hot,
I'd ne'er go to Owdham, boh i' Englond I'd stop;
It matters nowt, Madge, for to Owdham I'll go,
I'll naw clam to deeoth, boh sumbry shalt know:

Furst Frenchman I find, I'll tell him meh mind,
Un if he'll naw feight, he shall run.

Then down th' broo I coom, for we livent at top,
I thowt I'd reach Owdham ere ever I'd stop;
Ecod! heaw they stared when I getten to th' Mumps,
Meh owd hat i' my hond, un meh clogs full o' stumps;
Boh I soon towd um, I'r gooink to Owdham,
Un I'd ha'e a battle wi' th' French.

I kept eendway thro' th' lone, un to Owdham I went,
I εsh'd a recruit if te'd made up their keawnt?
No, no, honest lad, (for he tawked like a king),
Go wi' meh thro' the street, un thee I will bring
Where, if theaw'rt willink, theaw may ha'e a shillink.
Ecod! I thowt this wur rare news.

He browt me to th' pleck where te measurn their height,
Un if they bin height, there's nowt said about weight;
I retched me, un stretched me, un never did flinch,
Says th' mon, I believe theaw'rt meh lad to an inch:
I thowt this'll do, I'st ha'e guineas enow,
Ecod! Owdham, brave Owdham for me.

So fare thee weel, Grinfilt, a soger I'm made,
I'n getten new shoon, un a rare cockade;
I'll feight for Owd Englond os hard os I con,
Oather French, Dutch, or Spanish, to me it's o one,
I'll make 'em to stare like a new-started hare,
Un I'll tell 'em fro' Owdham I coom.

XXVIII.

Thornehagh-Moor Woods.

A CELEBRATED NORTHAMPTONSHIRE POACHERS' SONG.

NOTTINGHAMSHIRE was, in the olden day, famous in song for the
exploits of Robin Hood and his merry men. In our times the
reckless spirit and daring of the heroes of "the greenwood
tree" may be traced in the poachers of the county, who have
also found poets to proclaim and exult over *their* lawless exploits;
and in *Thornehagh-Moor woods* we have a specimen of one of these
rude, but mischievous and exciting lyrics. The air is beautiful,
and of a lively character. There is a prevalent idea that the
song is not the production of an ordinary ballad-writer, but was
written by a gentleman of rank and education, who, detesting the
English game-laws, adopted a too successful mode of inspiring
the peasantry with a love of poaching. The song finds locality
in the village of Thornehagh, in the hundred of Newark; the
common, or Moor-fields were inclosed about 1797, and are now
no longer called by the ancient designation. They contain eight
hundred acres. The manor of Thornehagh is the property of
the ancient family of Nevile, who have a residence on the estates.

In Thornehagh-Moor woods, in Nottinghamshire,
        Fol de rol, la re, right fol laddie, dee;
In Robin Hood's bold Nottinghamshire,
        Fol de rol, la re da.
Three keepers' houses stood three-square,
And about a mile from each other they were,—
Their orders were to look after the deer.
        Fol de rol, la re da.

I went out with my dogs one night,—
The moon shone clear, and the stars gave light;

Over hedges and ditches, and rails,
With my two dogs close at my heels,
To catch a fine buck in Thornehagh-Moor fields.

Oh! that night we had bad luck,
One of my very best dogs was stuck;
He came to me both bleeding and lame,—
Right sorry was I to see the same,—
He was not able to follow the game.

I searched his wounds, and found them slight,
Some keeper has done this out of spite;
Bnt I'll take my pike-staff,—that's the plan!
I'll range the woods till I find the man,
And I'll tan his hide right well,—if I can!

I ranged the woods and groves all night,
I ranged the woods till it proved daylight;
The very first thing that then I found,
Was a good fat buck, that lay dead on the ground;
I knew my dogs gave him his death-wound.

I hired a butcher to skin the game,
Likewise another to sell the same;
The very first buck he offered for sale,
Was to an old [hag] that sold bad ale,
And she sent us three poor lads to gaol.

The quarter sessions we soon espied,
At which we all were for to be tried;

The Chairman laughed the matter to scorn,
He said the old woman was all forsworn,
And unto pieces she ought to be torn.

The sessions are over, and we are clear!
The sessions are over, and we sit here,
   Singing fol de rol, la re da! .
The very best game I ever did see,
Is a buck or a deer, but a deer for me!
In Thornehagh-Moor woods this night we'll be!
   Fol de rol, la re da!

XXIX.

Somersetshire Hunting Song.

The following old song is popular with the peasantry of
Somersetshire.

There's no pleasures can compare
Wi' the hunting o' the hare,
In the morning, in the morning,
In fine and pleasant weather.
Chorus. With our hosses and our hounds,
   We will scamps it o'er the grounds,
   And sing traro, huzza!
   And sing traro, huzza!
   And sing traro, brave boys, we will foller.

And when poor puss arise,
Then away from us she flies;
And we'll gives her, boys, we'll gives her,
One thundering and loud holler!
 Cho. With our hosses, &c.

And when poor puss is killed,
We'll retires from the field;
And we'll count boys, and we'll count
On the same good ren to morrer.
  Chorus. With our hosses and our hounds, &c.

XXX.

𝕿𝖍𝖊 𝕾𝖊𝖊𝖉𝖘 𝖔𝖋 𝕷𝖔𝖛𝖊.

THIS very curious old song is not only a favourite with our peasantry, but, through its being introduced in the modern dramatic
entertainment of *The Loan of a Lover*, has obtained popularity
in more elevated circles. Its sweetly plaintive tune may be seen
in Chappell's *National English Airs.* The words are quaint, but
by no means void of beauty; they are, no doubt, corrupted, as
we have them in the common broadsides from which the editor is
obliged to print, not having been able to meet with them in any
other form.

I SOWED the seeds of love, it was all in the spring,
In April, May, and June, likewise, when small birds
   they do sing;
My garden's well planted with flowers every where,
Yet I had not the liberty to choose for myself the flower
   that I loved so dear.

My gardener he stood by, I asked him to choose for me,
He chose me the violet, the lilly and pink, but those I
   I refused all three;
The violet I forsook, because it fades so soon,
The lilly and the pink I did o'erlook, and I vowed I'd
   stay till June.

In June there's a red rose-bud, and that's the flower
    for me!
But often have I plucked at the red rose-bud till I
    gained the willow tree;   [twine,—
The willow-tree will twist, and the willow-tree will
O! I wish I was in the dear youth's arms that once
    had the heart of mine.

My gardener he stood by, he told me to take great care,
For in the middle of a red rose-bud there grows a sharp
    thorn there;
I told him I'd take no care till I did feel the smart,
And often I plucked at the red rose-bud till I pierced
    it to the heart.

I'll make me a posy of hyssop,—no other I can touch,—
That all the world may plainly see I love one flower
    too much;
My garden is run wild! where shall I plant anew—
For my bed, that once was covered with thyme, is all
    overrun with rue?

XXXI.

Pretty Sally's Answer.

CAREY'S song of *Sally in our Alley* has appeared in so many collections, that, notwithstanding its undying popularity, it has not
been deemed advisable to print it in the present work. The
Answer, however, is not so well known. It appeared immediately
after the publication of the original song, and in the broadside

called *Pretty Sally's Garland*, has invariably accompanied it. We cannot ascertain whether the *Answer* was written by Carey.

———

Of all the lads in London town,
　　There's none I love like Johnny;
He walks so stately o'er the ground,
　　I like him for my honey.
And none but him I e'er will wed,
　　As my name is Sally;
And I will dress me in my best,
　　In spite of all our alley.

Because that Nan and Sue did say,
　　That live in our alley,
Unto Bess Franklin, do but see,
　　Look, there goes pretty Sally!
But let them know, though they say so,
　　That I have store of money,
And can a hundred pounds bestow
　　On John, my dearest honey!

'Tis true my father deals in nets,
　　My mother in long laces;
But what of that? if Johnny's pleased,
　　'Twon't hinder our embraces.
For Johnny he does often swear
　　He dearly loves his Sally;
And for the neighbours I don't care,
　　We will live in our alley.

It's true, when Johnny comes along,
    And I by chance do meet him,
His master comes out with a stick,
    And sorely he doth beat him:
Yet Johnny shall be made amends,
    When his time's out, by Sally;
In spite of all the rogues and girls
    That live in our alley.

There is one day in every week
    That Johnny does come to me,
And then, I own, I am well pleased,
    When he doth kiss and woo me:
Then in the fields we walk and talk,—
    He calls me dearest Sally!
I love him, and I'll have him, too,
    In spite of all our alley.

His cheeks are of a crimson red,
    Black eye-brows he does carry;
His temper is so sweet and good,
    My Johnny I will marry.
Though all the neighbours spite us sore,
    Because Johnny loves his Sally,
I but love Johnny more and more,
    And a fig for all our alley!

Old women grumble, and the maids
    Are all in love with Johnny;

Q

But they may fume, and they may fret,
    For he'll not leave his honey:
At Midsummer his time is out,
    Then, hand-in-hand, will Sally
Unto the parson with him go,
    In spite of all our alley!

XXXII.

The Garden-gate.

THIS is one of the most pleasing of our rural ditties.   The air is
very beautiful.   The editor lately heard it sung in Malhamdale,
Yorkshire, by Willy Bolton, an old Dales'-minstrel, who accompanied himself on the union-pipes.

THE day was spent, the moon shone bright,
    The village clock struck eight;
Young Mary hastened, with delight,
    Unto the garden-gate:
But what was there that made her sad?—
The gate was there, but not the lad,
Which made poor Mary say and sigh,
Was ever poor girl so sad as I?

She traced the garden here and there,
    The village clock struck nine;
Which made poor Mary sigh, and say,
    You shan't, you shan't be mine!
You promised to meet at the gate at eight,
You ne'er shall keep me, nor make me wait,

For I'll let all such creatures see,
They ne'er shall make a fool of me.

She traced the garden here and there,
    The village clock struck ten ;
Young William caught her in his arms,
    No more to part again:
For he'd been to buy the ring that day,
And O! he had been a long, long way ;—
Then, how could Mary cruel prove,
To banish the lad she so dearly did love?

Up with the morning sun they rose,
    To church they went away,
And all the village joyful were,
    Upon their wedding-day:
Now in a cot, by a river side,
William and Mary both reside;
And she blesses the night, that she did wait
For her absent swain, at the garden-gate.

XXXIII.

The New-Mown Hay.

THIS song is a village-version of an incident which occurred in
the Burleigh family.   The same English adventure has, strangely
enough, been made the subject of one of the most beautiful of
Moore's *Irish Melodies*, viz., *You remember Helen, the hamlet's
pride.*

As I walked forth one summer's morn,
    Hard by a river's side,

Where yellow cowslips did adorn
    The blushing field with pride;
I spied a damsel on the grass,
    More blooming than the may;
Her looks the Queen of Love surpassed,
    Among the new-mown hay.

I said, good morning, pretty maid,
    How came you here so soon?
To keep my father's sheep, she said,
    The thing that must be done:
While they are feeding 'mong the dew,
    To pass the time away,
I sit me down to knit or sew,
    Among the new-mown hay.

Delighted with her simple tale,
    I sat down by her side;
With vows of love I did prevail
    On her to be my bride:
In strains of simple melody,
    She sung a rural lay;
The little lambs stood list'ning by,
    Among the new-mown hay.

Then to the church they went with speed,
    And Hymen joined them there;
No more her ewes and lambs to feed,
    For she's a lady fair:

A lord he was that married her,
　　To town they came straightway:
She may bless the day he spied her there,
　　Among the new-mown hay.

XXXIV.

The Summer's Morning.

This is a very old ditty, and a favourite with the peasantry in
every part of England; but more particularly with those in the
mining districts of the North.　The tune is pleasing, but uncom-
mon.　The editor's brother, R. W. Dixon, Esq., of Seaton-Carew,
Durham, by whom the song is communicated to our pages,
says, "I have written down the above, *verbatim*, as generally
sung.　It will be seen that the last lines of each verse are not of
equal length.　The singer, however, dexterously makes all right
and smooth!　The words underlined in each verse are sung five
times, thus:—*They ad-van-cèd, they ad-van-cèd, they ad-van·cèd, they
ad-van-cèd, they ad-van-cèd me some money,—ten guineas and a crown.*
The last line is thus sung:—*We'll be married,* (as the word is
usually pronounced), *We'll be married, we'll be married, we'll be married, we'll be married, we'll be married, we'll be mar-rì-èd when I
return again.*

It was one summer's morning, as I went o'er the moss,
I had no thought of 'listing, till the soldiers did me
　　cross;
They kindly did invite me to a flowing bowl, and down,
They advancèd me some money,—ten guineas and a
　　crown.

It's true my love has listed, he wears a white cockade,
He is a handsome young man, besides a roving blade;

He is a handsome young man, and he's gone to serve
         the king,
Oh! my very heart is breaking for the loss of him.

Oh! may he never prosper, oh! may he never thrive,
Nor anything he takes in hand so long as he's alive;
May the very grass he treads upon the ground refuse
         to grow,
Since he's been the only cause of my sorrow, grief, and
         woe!

Then he pullèd out a handkerchief to wipe her flow-
         ing eyes,
Leave off those lamentations, likewise those mournful
         cries;
Leave off those lamentations, while I march o'er the
         plain,
We'll be married when I return again.

XXXV.

Old Adam.

The editor has had some trouble in procuring a copy of this
old song, which used, in his boyish days, to be very popular
with aged people resident in the North of England. It has been,
however, long out of print, and handed down traditionally. By
the kindness of Mr. S. Swindells, printer, Manchester, he has been
favoured with an ancient printed copy, which Mr. Swindells
observes he had great difficulty in meeting with.

Both sexes give ear to my fancy,
     While in praise of dear woman I sing;

Confined not to Moll, Sue, or Nancy,
   But mates from a beggar to king.

When old Adam first was created,
   And lord of the universe crowned,
His happiness was not completed,
   Until that an helpmate was found.

He'd a garden so planted by nature,
   Man cannot produce in his life;
But yet the all-wise Creator
   Still saw that he wanted a wife.

Then Adam he laid in a slumber,
   And there he lost part of his side;
And when he awoke, with great wonder,
   Beheld his most beautiful bride!

In transport he gazèd upon her,
   His happiness now was complete!
He praisèd his bountiful donor,
   Who thus had bestowed him a mate.

She was not took out of his head, sir,
   To reign and triumph over man;
Nor was she took out of his feet, sir,
   By man to be trampled upon.

But she was took out of his side, sir,
   His equal and partner to be;

But as they are united in one, sir,
   The man is the top of the tree.

Then let not the fair be despisèd
   By man, as she's part of himself;
For woman by Adam was prizèd
   More than the whole globe full of wealth.

Man, without a woman's a beggar,
   Suppose the whole world he possest;
And the beggar that's got a good woman,
   With more than the world he is blest.

<hr>

XXXVI.

Trelawny.

THIS spirited song was written at the time of the committal of
Bishop Trelawny to the Tower, in 1688, for his defence of the
Protestant religion. He was then Bishop of Bristol, but in the
same year was made Bishop of Exeter, and in 1707 was translated
to the See of Winchester. The song has been handed down traditionally since 1688, and has never appeared in print, except in
a work of limited circulation edited by the late Davies Gilbert.

<hr>

A GOOD sword, and a trusty hand,
   A merry heart, and true!
King James's men shall understand
   What Cornish men can do.

And have they fixed the where, and when?
   And shall Trelawny die?
Then twenty thousand Cornish men
   Will know the reason why!

Out spake the captain, brave and bold,—
    A merry wight was he ;
Though London Tower were Michael's hold,
    We'll set Trelawny free.

We'll cross the Tamar, land to land,
    The Severn is no stay;
And side by side, and hand in hand,
    And who shall bid us nay?

And when we come to London wall,
    A pleasant sight to view;
Come forth! come forth! ye cowards, all,
    Here are better men than you!

Trelawny he's in keep in hold;
    Trelawny he may die!
But twenty thousand Cornish bold,
    Will know the reason why !

XXXVII.

Tobacco.

This song is a mere adaptation of a portion of the Rev. Ebenezer
Erskine's poem *Smoking Spiritualized*, which we have given at
page 37 of the present work. The earliest copy of the abridg-
ment with which we have been able to meet, is the one in
D'Urfey's *Pills to purge Melancholy*, 1719, but whether we are
indebted for it to the original author, or to "that bright genius,
Tom D'Urfey," as Burns calls him, we are not able to determine.
The song has always been popular.

    Tobacco's but an Indian weed,
    Grows green in the morn, cut down at eve;

It shows our decay,
We are but clay;
Think of this when you smoke tobacco!

The pipe that is so lilly white,
Wherein so many take delight,
It's broken with a touch,—
Man's life is such;
Think of this when you take tobacco!

The pipe that is so foul within,
It shows man's soul is stained with sin;
It doth require
To be purged with fire;
Think of this when you smoke tobacco!

The dust that from the pipe doth fall,
It shews we are nothing but dust at all;
For we came from the dust,
And return we must;
Think of this when you smoke tobacco!

The ashes that are left behind,
Do serve to put us all in mind
That into dust
Return we must;
Think of this when you take tobacco!

The smoke that does so high ascend,
Shews that man's life must have an end;

The vapour's gone,—
Man's life is done;
Think of this when you take tobacco !

———

XXXVIII.

𝕿𝖍𝖊 𝕾𝖕𝖆𝖓𝖎𝖘𝖍 𝕷𝖆𝖉𝖎𝖊𝖘.

THIS song is ancient, but we have no means of ascertaining at what period it was written. Captain Marryatt, in his novel of *Poor Jack*, introduces it, and says it is *old*. It is a general favourite. The air is plaintive, and in the minor key.

———

FAREWELL, and adieu to you Spanish ladies,
  Farewell, and adieu to you ladies of Spain !
For we've received orders for to sail for old England,
  But we hope in a short time to see you again.

We'll rant and we'll roar like true British heroes,
  We'll rant and we'll roar across the salt seas,
Until we strike soundings in the channel of old England;
  From Ushant to Scilly is thirty-five leagues.

Then we hove our ship to, with the wind at sou'-west,
    boys,
  We hove our ship to, for to strike soundings clear;
We got soundings in ninety-five fathom, and boldly
  Up the channel of old England our course we did steer.

The first land we made it was callèd the Deadman,
    Next, Ram'shead off Plymouth, Start, Portland,
       and Wight;
We passèd by Beechy, by Fairleigh, and Dungeness,
    And hove our ship to, off the South Foreland light.

Then a signal was made for the grand fleet to anchor,
    All in the downs, that night for to sleep;
Then stand by your stoppers, let go your shank-painters,
    Haul all your clew-garnets, stick out tacks and sheets.

So let every man toss off a full bumper,
    Let every man toss off his full bowls;
We'll drink and be jolly, and drown melancholy,
    So here's a good health to all true-hearted souls!

XXXIX.

The Tars of the Blanche.

THIS song, though rather advanced in years, has not arrived at an
age sufficient to entitle it to be called an *ancient* one; and the
editor, therefore, was in doubt whether he should insert it; but,
from its popularity, as well as from its poetical merit, he is
induced to yield to the solicitation of numerous friends and
supporters of the PERCY SOCIETY who will not be satisfied
if it be omitted. It is a street-ballad, and written by some
unknown author. The first time we heard it sung was by a
charcoal-burner in the New Forest. It was a hot sultry summer's day in 1835, and tired with pedestrianing, we had just
entered a small inn when our ears were regaled with the *Tars of
the Blanche.* The swarthy songster gave it with great spirit, and

the chorus was well sustained, by five or six fine-looking fellows
of the like occupation with himself.

———

You Frenchmen, don't boast of your fighting,
    Nor talk of your deeds on the main;
Do you think that old England you'll frighten,
    As easy as Holland or Spain?
We listen and laugh while you threaten, —
    We fear not your wily advance;
The boasting Le Picque has been taken
    By the jolly brave tars of the Blanche!

We sailed from the Bay of Point Peter,
    Four hundred and fifty on board;
We were all ready to meet them,
    To conquer or die, was the word!
While the can of good liquor was flowing,
    We gave them three cheers to advance,
And courage in each heart was glowing,—
    For cowards ne'er sailed in the Blanche!

The night then advancing upon us,
    The moon did afford us a light;
Each star then with lustre was shining,
    To keep the French frigates in sight:
While the night-breeze our sails fillèd gently,
    Our ship through the water did launch;
And the grog flew about in full bumpers,
    Among the brave tars of the Blanche.

The fight made the sea seem on fire,
    Each bullet distractedly flew;
Britannia her sons did inspire
    With courage, that damped the French crew:
Saying, Cowards now surely must rue,—
    While over them Death turned his lance,
Our balls did repeat, as they flew,
    Fight on, my brave tars of the Blanche!

When Falkner resigned his last breath,
    Each gave a deep groan and a sigh;
Such sorrow was found at his death,
    And tears fell from every eye.
Like Wolfe, then with victory crowned,
    At his death he cried, ne'er mind my chance,
But, like gallant heroes, fight on,
    Or expire by the name of the Blanche!

Stout Wilkins his place soon supplied,
    And like a bold actor engaged;
And his guns with more judgment to guide,
    By the loss of his captain enraged.
And who could his fury allay,
    When Le Picque alongside did advance?
For our masts being all shot away,
    We grappled her close to the Blanche!

Our foremast and mizen being gone,
    The French thought to make us their own!
And while *Vive la Republique!* they sung,—
    I thought that they ne'er would have done:

We joinèd their song with dismay,
　　And music that made them to dance;
And not a false note did we play,—
　　The harmonious tars of the Blanche!

When they found it in vain for to stand,
　　They cried out for quarter amain;
Although the advantage they had,
　　Still Britons are lords of the main!
So push round the grog, let it pass!
　　Since they've found us true-hearted and staunch;
Each lad with his favourite lass,
　　Drink success to the tars of the Blanche!

FINIS.

NOTES.

P. 5, l. 15.—Ere thou canst say " they're gone."] This line is printed as we found it, but the meaning seems obscured by the inverted commas. We would read the line as a parenthesis, and use the word *say* in the signification of *speak,* or *utter an expression.*

P. 22, l. 24.—Grub.] An early instance of a cant term still used in the same sense.

P. 42.—A Dialogue between the Husband-man and the Serving-man.] In the third volume of the Roxburgh Collection is an ancient black-letter copy of this curious production It is without date, or printer's name, and varies, but not materially, from our version. We give the title and rhyming argument.—" *God speed the Plow, and bless the Corn-mow; a Dialogue between the Husband-man and the Serving-man.*

> " The Serving-man the Plow-man would invite
> To leave his calling, and to take delight ;
> But he to that by no means will agree,
> Lest he thereby should come to beggary :
> He makes it plain appear a country life
> Doth far excell,—and so they end their strife.

—The tune is, I am the Duke of Norfolk."

P. 52.   The late Francis King.] This poor minstrel, from whose recitation two of our ballads were obtained, met his

R

death by drowning, in December 1844. He had been at a merry-making at Gargrave, in Craven, and it is supposed that, owing to the darkness of the night, he had mistaken his homeward road, and walked into the water. He was one in whose character were combined the mime and the minstrel ; and his old jokes, and older ballads and songs, ever insured him a hearty welcome. His appearance was peculiar, and, owing to one leg being shorter than its companion, he walked in such a manner as once drew from a wag the remark " that few *Kings* had had more ups and downs in the world !" As a musician, his talents were creditable, and some of the dance-tunes that he was in the habit of composing, shewed that he was not deficient in the organ of melody. In the quiet church-yard of Gargrave may be seen the minstrel's grave.

> " Aye, there he rests !—
> There, where the daisy lifts its modest head
> Above the trefoil green ;—where glides the Aire,
> Lapsing along in liquid music, far
> O'er the romantic land he loved so well !"

P. 57, l. 7.—*Queen.*] Quære, quean ?

P. 58, l. 11.—*Meet.*] This word seems used in the sense of the French verb *mettre*, to put, or place.

P. 71.—*The Bold Pedlar and Robin Hood.*] Though, as we have stated, this ballad is not in any collection, the subject is the same as that of the old ballad called *Robin Hood newly reviv'd: or the Meeting and Fighting with his Cousin Scarlet.* *Vide* Evans's *Old Ballads,* and Ritson's *Robin Hood.*

P. 73, l. 21.—*Gamble Gold.*] The stall copies read Gamble bold.

P. 74.—*The Outlandish Knight.*] In the Roxburgh Collection is a copy of this ballad, in which the catastrophe is brought about in a different manner. When the young lady finds that she is to be drowned, she very leisurely makes a particular examination of the place of her intended execution, and raises an objection to some nettles which are growing on the banks of the stream! these she requires to be removed, in the following very poetical manner:—

> " Go fetch the sickle, to crop the nettle,
>   That grows so near the brim ;
>   For fear it should tangle my golden locks,
>   Or freckle my milk-white skin."

A request so elegantly made, is gallantly complied with by the treacherous knight, who, while engaged in " cropping," is pushed into the stream, and meets the just reward of his perfidy!

P. 80.—*Lord Delaware.*] The editor has recently met with a homely version of this ballad.

P. 89, l. 10.—*pine.*] Grief.

P. 102, l. 16.—*Fight wi' me.*] *i.e.* along with me.

P. 104, l. 9.—*Fankit.*] Sheathed, or confined.

P. 109.—*The King and the Tinkler.*] The late Robert Anderson, the Cumbrian bard, in his song of the *Clay Daubin*, represents Deavie as singing *The King and the Tinkler*.

> " He lilted *The King and the Tinkler*,
>   And Wully strack up *Robin Hood ;*
>   Dick Mingins tried *Hooly and Fairly*,
>   And Martha the *Babs o' the Wood.*"

P. 112.—*The Keach i' the Creel.*] *i. e.* the catch in the basket.

P. 126.—*Saddle to Rags.*] Since we inserted this highwayman's *ballad*, we have been favoured by a correspondent with a highwayman's song, which looks like a composition of the reign of Charles II. From the carelessness of

printers the copy abounded with mistakes, which so obscure
the meaning, that we could not have inserted it in the state
in which it came to our hands.   The following is the song
alluded to, but it is given with several conjectural emenda-
tions, made by a friend who is better acquainted with such
pop-ular literature than the editor.

THE TROTTING HORSE.

I CAN sport as fine a trotting horse as any swell in town,
To trot you fourteen miles an hour, I'll bet you fifty crown;
He is such a one to bend his knees, and tuck his haunches in,
And throw the dust in people's face, and think it not a sin.
          For to ride away, trot away,
            Ri, fa lar, la, &c.

He has an eye like any hawk, a neck like any swan,
A foot light as the stag's, the while his back is scarce a span;
Kind Nature hath so formed him, he is everything that's good,—
Aye! everything a man could wish, in bottom, bone, and blood.
          For to ride away, &c.

If you drop the rein, he'll nod his head, and boldly walk away,
While others kick and bounce about, to him it's only play;
There never was a finer horse e'er went on English ground,
He is rising six years old, and is all over right and sound.
          For to ride away, trot away, &c.

If any frisk or milling match should call me out of town,
I can pass the blades with white cockades, their whiskers hanging down;
With large jack-towels round their necks, they think they're first and fast,
But, with their gapers open wide, they find that they are last.
          Whilst I ride away, trot away, &c.

If threescore miles I am from home, I darkness never mind,
My friend is gone, and I am left, with pipe and pot behind;
Up comes some saucy kiddy, a scampsman on the hot,
But ere he pulls the trigger I am off just like a shot.
          For I ride away, trot away, &c.

If Fortune e'er should fickle be, and wish to have again
That which she so freely gave, I'd give it without pain :
I would part with it right freely, and without the least remorse,
Only grant to me what God hath gave, my mistress and my horse !
       That I may ride away, trot away, &c.

P. 128, l. 2.—*Ghyll.*] A narrow rocky valley branching out of one of the larger mountain-dales or passes. The word ghyll, or gill, or giel, is used in the same sense in Iceland and Norway. The name of the tremendous Norwegian pass, *Vettie's Giel*, described by so many English travellers, will occur to our readers.

P. 165, l. 9.—*Parkin.*] A cake composed of oatmeal, carraway-seeds, and treacle; "ale and parkin" is a common morning-meal in the North of England.

P. 168, l. 20.—*'Twas all his daily* prise.] This word should have been printed 'prise, to show that it was an abbreviation of emprise;—an hazardous attempt.

P. 171.—*The Farmer's Son.*] This song is found in *The Vocal Miscellany; a Collection of above four hundred celebrated Songs,* the first edition of which was published in 1729. As the *Miscellany* makes no pretension to anything beyond a "Collection," we may fairly presume the song to be of anterior date to 1729.

P. 173.—*Wooing Song of a Yeoman of Kent's Sonne.*] We have here the original of a well-known Scottish song.—

    " I hae laid a herring in saut ;
       Lass, gin ye lo'e me, tell me now !
    I hae brew'd a forpet o' maut,
       An' I canna come ilka day to woo !"

P. 175.—*Harvest Home Song.*] A copy of this song, with the music, may be found in D'Urfey's *Pills to purge Melancholy.* It varies from our's, but we have not adopted its renderings. D'Urfey's work has been greatly overrated; so far as the music is concerned, it *may* be an authority; but he took such liberties with the text of the songs, that we would sooner trust to a modern broadside, or even to a traditional version, than to his book.

P. 178.—*The Barley-Mow Song.*] The Suffolk peasantry have the following very short version of the *Barley-Mow Song:*—

> " Here's a health to the barley mow !
>   Here's a health to the man
>   Who very well can
> Both harrow, and plough, and sow !
>
> " When it is well sown,
>   See it is well mown,—
>   Both raked and gavelled clean,
>   And a barn to lay it in.
>   Here's a health to the man
>   Who very well can
> Both thrash, and fan it clean !"

P. 185, l. 16—*Sellenger's Round.*] The common modern copies read *St. Leger's Round.*

P. 196, l. 10.—*Trunk weam.*—Taken in the literal sense, this would mean trunk, or box-belly. It is evidently a cant term for a fiddle.

P. 196.—*The Maskers' Song.*] Robert Kearton, a working miner, and librarian and lecturer at the Grassington Mechanics' Institution, informs us that at Coniston, in Lancashire, and the neighbourhood, the maskers go about at the proper season, viz., Easter. Their introductory song is different to the one given by us. He has favoured us with two verses of the delectable composition ; he says, " I dare say they'll be quite sufficient !"

> " The next that comes on
>   Is a gentleman's son ;—
> A gentleman's son he was born ;

> For mutton and beef,
> You may look at his teeth,
> He's a laddie for picking a bone!

> " The next that comes on
> Is a tailor so bold,—
> He can stitch np a hole in the dark !
> There's never a 'prentice
> In famed London city,
> Can find any fault with his *wark!!*

P. 201.—*Richard of Taunton Dean.*] As an exemplifi-
cation of the extensive popularity which this old West-
country ditty has obtained, the editor has been favoured by
T. Crofton Croker, Esq. with two Irish versions. One of
them is entitled, *Last New-Year's Day*, and is printed by
Haly, Hanover Street, Cork. It is almost verbatim with the
English song, with the exception of the first and second
verses, which are as follows:—

> " Last New-Year's Day, as I heard say,
> Dick mounted on his dapple gray ;
> He mounted high and he mounted low,
> Until he came to *sweet Raphoe !*
> Sing fal de dol de ree,
> Fol de dol, righ fol dee.

> " My buckskin does I did put on,
> My spladdery clogs, *to save my brogues !*
> And in my pocket a lump of bread,
> And round my hat a ribbon red."

The other version is entitled *Dicky of Ballyman*, and a
note informs us that " *Dicky of Ballyman's sirname
was Byrne !*" As our readers may like to hear how the
Somersetshire bumpkin behaved after he had located
himself in the town of Ballyman, and taken the sirname of
Byrne, we give the whole of his amatory adventures in the

sister-island. We discover from them, *inter alia*, that he had found the "best of friends" in his "Uncle,"—that he had made a grand discovery in natural history, viz., that a rabbit is a *fowl!*—that he had taken the temperance pledge, which, however, his Mistress Ann had certainly *not* done; and, moreover, that he had become an enthusiast in potatoes!

DICKY OF BALLYMAN.

"On New-Year's Day, as I heard say,
Dicky he saddled his dapple gray;
He put on his Sunday clothes,
His scarlet vest, and his new made hose.
    Diddle dum di, diddle dum do,
    Diddle dum di, diddle dum do.

"He rode till he came to Wilson Hall,
There he rapped, and loud did call;
Mistress Ann came down straightway,
And asked him what he had to say?

"Don't you know me, Mistress Ann?
I am Dicky of Ballyman;
An honest lad, though I am poor,—
I never was in love before.

"I have an uncle, the best of friends,
Sometimes to me a fat rabbit he sends;
And many other dainty fowl,
To please my life, my joy, my *soul.*   (*sowl*)

"Sometimes I reap, sometimes I mow,
And to the market I do go,
To sell my father's corn and hay,—
I earn my sixpence every day!

"Oh, Dicky! you go beneath your mark,—
You only wander in the dark;
Sixpence a day will never do,
I must have silks, and satins, too!

" Besides, Dicky, I must have *tea* (*tay*)
  For my breakfast, every day ;
  And after dinner a bottle of wine,—
  For without it I cannot dine.

" If on fine clothes our money is spent,
  Pray how shall my lord be paid his rent ?
  He'll expect it when 'tis due,—
  Believe me, what I say is true.

" As for tea, good stirabout
  Will do far better, I make no doubt;
  And spring water, when you dine,
  Is far wholesomer than wine.

" Potatoes, too, are very nice food,—
  I don't know any half so good :
  You may have them boiled or roast,
  Whichever way you like them most.

" This gave the company much delight,
  And made them all to laugh outright;
  So Dicky had no more to say,
  But saddled his dapple and rode away.
        Diddle dum di, &c."

In concluding these remarks, we may just observe that
we lately heard an old Yorkshire yeoman sing *Richard of
Taunton Dean*, who commenced his version with this fine
line :—

    " It was at the time of a high holiday."

P. 203, l. 23.—*Doat-fig*.] A fig newly gathered from the
tree, so called to distinguish it from a grocer's, or preserved
fig.

P. 206.—*Joan's Ale was New*.] This song is mentioned
in *Thackeray's Catalogue* under the title of *Jone's Ale's New*.
Thackeray began to publish about nineteen years after the
Commonwealth, so that the circumstantial evidence is
strongly in favour of the hypothesis advanced in our introductory remarks.

P. 215, l. 13.—*Bane.*] Near.

Ibid.—*Town-gate.*] The high-road through a town or village.

Ibid. l. 20.—*But 'twor Tommy opinion.*] *i. e.* Tommy's opinion. In the Yorkshire dialect, where the possessive case is followed by the relative substantive, it is customary to omit the *s*, but if the relative be understood, and not expressed, the possessive case is formed in the usual manner, as in a subsequent line of the same song.—

" He'd a horse, too, twar war than oud *Tommy's*, ye see."

Ibid. l. 26.—*Swop.*] Exchange.

Ibid. l. 26.—*Wick.*] ·Alive, quick.

P. 216, l. 1.—*Nobbut.*] Only.

P. 217, l. 16.—*Clemmink.*] Famished. The line in which this word occurs exhibits one of the most striking peculiarities of the Lancashire dialect, which is, that in words ending in *ing*, the termination is changed into *ink*. *Ex. gr.* for starving, *starvink*, farthing, *fardink*.

P. 231, l. 20.—*To reign and triumph.*] Quære, should we not read "to triumph and reign."

P. 233, l. 3.—*Michael's hold.*] The fortress on St. Michael's Mount, Cornwall.

P. 235, l. 15.—*We'll rant and we'll roar.*] These words have, in modern copies, been changed into, *We'll range and we'll rove*, but our reading is correct ; the phrase occurs in several old songs.

*** *Richard of Taunton Dean.*] In the fourth edition of Halliwell's *Nursery Rhymes of England*, which has just issued from the press, we observe a version of this song, called *Richard of Dalton Dale.*

FINIS.